MANHANDLED
"Hidden Code Words That Impact Men And The People That Love Them"

Dr. OLIVER T. REID

If you purchased this book without a cover you should be aware that this book is stolen property. It was reported as "unsold and destroyed" to the publisher, and the author has not received payment for this "stripped book".

Copyright © 2016 Author Dr. Oliver T. Reid

Published by- Publishing For Pastors

All rights reserved.

ISBN: 1530563844
ISBN-13: 978-1530563845

All rights reserved. Except for use in the case of brief quotations embodied in critical articles and reviews, the reproduction or utilization of this work in whole or part in any form by any electronic, digital, mechanical or other means, now known or hereafter invented, including xerography, photocopying, scanning, recording, or any information storage or retrieval system, is forbidden without prior written permission of the author and publisher.

The scanning, uploading, and distribution of this book via the Internet or via any other means without permission of the publisher and author is illegal and punishable by law. Purchase only authorized versions of this book and do not participate in or encourage electronic piracy of copyrighted materials. Your support of the author's rights is appreciated.

Scripture Quotations are taken from the King James Version of the Bible, AMP
Version copyright 1973, 1978, 1984 by the International Bible Society.
Used by Permission of Zondervan Publishing House. All rights reserved.

For ordering, booking, permission, questions, or interviews, contact the author.

Printed in the United States of America
First Printing 2016

Edited by: Shantae A. Charles for GOD Ideas, LLC
Cover Design: Fernando Palacios
(I AM A SOLUTION CONSULTING FIRM, LLC)

Foreword

MAN-UFACTURED

(MASCULINE DEVELOPEMENT)

The term "**manufactured**" means the making or producing of anything or the generating of something. Most, if not all, relationship literature that we read usually teaches women about the externalities of a men, but I would like to take an investigative approach to see men from the inside out.

Genesis 1:26 states, "Then God said "Let Us make man in our image according to Our likeness". Manufactured is a word derived from the Biblical concept of man being created by God. The original intent for manhood has been grossly perverted to mean something totally opposite of man's original purpose. Ladies, I would like take you on a journey into God's mind when He made your man.

The term "**anatomy**" means a study of the structure or internal workings of something. Please understand that man was created with the following foundational needs:

1. **SELF-RESPECT** - Men must sense honor and personal distinctiveness.

2. **THE ABILITY TO EXERCISE POWER** - Men have the need to

conquer things or enforce a standard.

3. **PURPOSE AND MEANING** - Men want to know that what they do has meaning to the people they love.

4. **INTIMACY AND COMPANIONSHIP** - Men want to be loved, understood and accepted by the ones they love.

As we look deeper into the personhood of man, here's what men connect with:

1. Men connect with parental contact and basic trust.

2. Men connect with peers and the ability to trust others.

3. Men connect sexually with the ability to be trusted and communicate specific emotions.

Ladies, this may not seem like your man, but it is in his core. Study these dynamics and cultivate an attitude conducive for the enhancement these foundational needs. God knew man needed special help because He stated, "It is not good for the man to alone; I will make him a helper [and completer] suitable for him" *(Genesis 2:18)*.

Whether you realize it or not, understand this ladies: men go through cycles and seasons. There are four seasons that men go through:

1. **SEASON OF MAN** – In this season, men face their weaknesses and overcome their fears.

2. **SEASON OF OX** – This is season is when men become productive.

MANHANDLED

"Hidden Code Words That Impact Men And The People That Love Them"

Much increase is by the strength of the "ox". An ox is a powerful animal. In early ancient Israel, the ox was the single most valuable animal one could own. The ox was the animal used to plow and to turn a mill or to do much of the heavy work that has to be done.

3. <u>**SEASON OF THE EAGLE**</u> - This is the season when men begin soaring in the Spirit. In this season men become high achievers, visionaries, and majestic leaders.

4. <u>**SEASON OF THE LION**</u> – *It is in this season when* **men become the king in his** God-given territory. The man in **this season is a** conqueror; he is overcoming; he walks in boldness; he is a warrior that seeks transformation and he walks in victory.

Apostle Kevin Graham

Founder and President of the Samuel Generation Training Center. Charlotte, NC

ACKNOWLEDGEMENTS & CONTRIBUTIONS

I would like to personally thank every man that dared to pause for a moment to add their valuable and timeless contribution to this book project. Many were called but you were chosen and responded to the sound of sharing your hearts with the world. Words will never be able to scratch the surface of what this not only means to me but to the man or woman that will lay eyes on this book. Contributing Authors, you men are infallible proof that I truly walk among the giants of this generation.

I would like to recognize men around the globe that have spoken through code words that their love ones couldn't or refused to decode. This book is dedicated to you. To the masses of men who have smiled through pain, cried with their eyes dry, laughed through misery, castrated by the words of others but standing erected, fathered though abandonment, and standing through life's battle scars, you are the heartbeat and anthem behind this book. I want that man to know I hear your screams from the silent places.

Dr. Oliver T. Reid

MANHANDLED

"Hidden Code Words That Impact Men And The People That Love Them"

"We're living in an age when male masculinity is under constant attack. However, Dr. Oliver T. Reid has written a book that will deal with the struggles of manhood and will give us sound advice to keep us on the course. "No sooner than a male child pushes his way out of his mother's womb, the battle starts. The battle is over power, authority and dominion. If his power has gone uncheck, it can be very detrimental to his well-being. What he needs is accountability, and to be investigated by the strength of other men. As a child growing up without a father; I was well on my way to a life totally contrary to the boundaries of home. Although my mother raised her eight children to be upright, the streets were more enticing than her rules. If it weren't for her pressuring me into attending church, the outcome would have been different today. I have had the misfortunes of burying three brothers because they didn't have anyone to check them when the pressure was turned up. They needed strong men to validate their masculinity and to show them a better way. I was able to escape the vicious cycle of death because of my willingness to associate myself with strong male figures and prayer. I thank God for His saving grace!

Pastor Johnny E. Brown II

Senior Pastor Rhema Covenant Worship Center International Harrisburg, NC

Who mentors the mentor? For years I extended my life to other boys and men in efforts to help and assist them in their endeavors in life. I considered myself a mentor (a trusted advisor who allowed boys and men to extract wisdom, knowledge and assistance directly from my life). As a mentor, I wanted to make sure these individuals were supported in their efforts to live successfully and accomplish goals. I spent hours on the phone, days traveling, weeks helping out planning in attempts to make sure my mentee's were properly mentored. As time progressed I sometime found myself seeking the assistance from a trusted advisor that I was giving to others. Truth of the matter, as a mentor, I gave others what I really desired myself (a mentor). When I did not always receive what I was giving in the

MANHANDLED

"Hidden Code Words That Impact Men And The People That Love Them"

natural, I concluded, according to the Law of Reciprocity, as I gave to others…God in return gave back to me.

Dr. Kedrick T. Lowery, Sr. Pastor

Grace Church of Durham
1417 Cole Mill Road
Durham, NC 27705
www.graceofdurham.org
Facebook - Grace of Durham
Twitter
Instagram

In order to develop MANHOOD MOMENTUM you will need to embrace the reality that COMPETENCE and CONFIDENCE is required. Competence deals with what you know and Confidence deals with knowing you, your worth, your purpose and believing in yourself. MANHOOD MOMENTUM happens as you remain committed to gaining greater levels of competency and as you remain committed to growing in your personal confidence. In Hebrews, Paul writes, "Cast not away therefore your confidence, which hath great recompense of reward." (Hebrews 10:35 KJV) What you know and how you flow will always push you forward into MANHOOD MOMENTUM that makes you fruitful in every area of your life.

John Wesley Pace II

John Pace Enterprises LLC
johnpace@johnpaceenterprises.com
www.johnpaceenterprises.com

First let me say that being a man is a honorable task, we have a great responsible to carry out the call and visions the Lord gives us. What were some of the challenges I had to face as a man going through my masculinity? The first challenge was trying to figure out my identity as a man. Who was I? Who was my father? Why did God form me in my mother's womb? Why did I have an unbalance childhood life? I will give you the short version of my masculinity life challenges.

It has always been God's will and desires for a child to grow up and be nurtured in a godly home. We know the devil and his partners in crime try to destroy, steal and kill God's plans for the godly family. He will try to have parents to divorce and leave kids in the home with only one parent who will have to raise the child

MANHANDLED

"Hidden Code Words That Impact Men And The People That Love Them"

by themselves and do homework with them and cook dinner, etc. Then they will only have little time for themselves, and lack self-care to deal with pain, stress, hurt, and anger toward the other parent because they feel alone in their tasks of raising a family.

So we must get our identity together to find out that we are men built to endure hardness as a good soldier no matter if we were taught or raised by one or two parents. I know the first hand of being confused about manhood. I had to overcome my struggle of who I was as a man. I had to deal with molestation as a 10 year old child. Growing up, I was confused for so many years but through God's guidance and help, He ordered my steps to meet a friend in high school whose Dad was a deacon and he invited me to their church. I got saved there at the age of nineteen and I've been running since, never looking back.

It was very hard to walk as a man at nineteen and I was struggling with my identity: a man or a woman? I was battling with things in my soul, knowing I was a man but was touched as a child inappropriately. So when I look back over my life it was the devil's plan to try to stop the call God had on my life but by the prayers and the Word of God, I made it and I'm still running for the things of God. He forgave me of much so I love him much knowing it was his grace and tender mercy that kept me when I was learning His Word and way of being a Christian.

We must not give up on life. We are men for a purpose and reason and that purpose is to be an example to young men who need to know that no matter what happens to you, or what the enemy tries to do we can make it even if we will come in on broken pieces.

The key to my manhood is this: I'm still alive. Remember: as long as you're breathing you still have hope and a chance to finish the task. You can get back up, you can find a job, you can find your kids to tell them you love them, no matter if you are in prison. You can still love them, write them and pray for them behind bars, so if you are alive you can rebuild and overcome the past mistakes. I'm a true witness that God's grace is sufficient and he will give you the victory. So the tools to get back up are to pray, read, write, hang around strong godly men, stay focused, have a true friend you

MANHANDLED

"Hidden Code Words That Impact Men And The People That Love Them"

can shared your struggle with and pray with others. Stay connected to a good Bible teaching church.

Your Brother in Christ,

Prophet Raymond Wilson
Charlotte, NC
raywilson948@gmail.com

Many people know Dr. Joe Shepard, the speaker, international author, and philanthropist, but back home they call me Pastor Lilly's grandson. My family was an extremely influential force in the march for spiritual liberation in South Jamaica Queens, NY. I would grow up to be one of those their legacy was committed to save. I understood the love of God and how to love my neighbor, how to respect my elders and how to serve in the church. Later in life, these values wouldn't seem like enough. I was in search of more than what I knew. I excelled in music and sought refuge on the stage in the pillows of the crowd. I studied the Scriptures and sought salvation in my prowess in religious anthropology. I was teaching and facilitating a fascination that was not my reality. I knew about the Gospel –but not about love. I knew the motions of love. I knew what love felt like, but I didn't know what it was like to have it within –because I did not know how to love myself.

After a sexual addiction ruined the integrity of my marriage, I was forced to confront the fear of the glooming cloud of clarity. I had been popular my entire career. I had learned more lessons than I had enough time to teach, but for the first time in life, I was alone. In the middle of a divorce, with my finances and possessions being divided like chores, I was left with only the memories of what I thought was all that life had to offer. I struggled with the notion of gaining all I had lost and maintaining my influence with no more spoils to share.

I realized that I was committed to the image of success more than my own happiness. One night –while asleep in my car, I was determined that my value would not be reduced to the money I had in my wallet. I was more than my credit score and vowed to be more than I had ever been. This time, it wouldn't be for the

MANHANDLED

"Hidden Code Words That Impact Men And The People That Love Them"

accolades or the congregation's applause. I would rise because I had more to offer than what people knew. Deep in the ruins of pride and rubble of my ministerial success, I found love.

After embracing the humility that comes to remind us all of our purpose, I would vow to remain committed on the posture of my faith. Today, I live in the moments I thought I would never see. I've learned how to use wealth to leverage my witness of God's love. It is the advantage of acknowledging the legacy of Christ that I understood: *We can only love others as we love ourselves.*

Dr. Joe Shepard, International Author, and Philanthropist

Founder and CEO of the Transformational Leadership Conference Inc.

When I was much younger, one of the biggest challenges of my masculinity was the PRESSURE that I felt on me to be a MAN. On the streets of Washington, D.C. is where I spent most of my life until age 26 when I became a Christian. As a young black man being groomed by the streets, there was big time pressure to be manly and to be accepted as a man by others. I have discovered that manhood for me was to understand my responsibilities, obligations, duties, and to fulfill them as faithfully as I could.

That meant sometimes I came up short of my OWN expectations & goals. But coming up short never meant failure to me. It means I missed this time but I will learn and grow from it to do better the next time around. I believe that I could equip other men with knowledge that I have learned from experience, trial and error. The bottom line for me, I would say is for me to be me, not trying to be a people pleaser. But for me to do, perform and fulfill all that I believe is my responsibility and duty as a man. If I was to sum up manhood in one sentence, I would say: A man handles his business and responsibilities with integrity, character and ethics.

Pastor Frank Owens, Jr
The Word of God Christian Center
Washington, DC

MANHANDLED

"Hidden Code Words That Impact Men And The People That Love Them"

On my 7th birthday, I had just hung up the phone with my biological father. He told me to keep an eye out for the UPS guy because he had shipped my present. Needless to say, my present never arrived. That event shaped my life as a man more than I realized. I felt dejected, tossed out like trash. Eventually I began to shut down. I became very angry, and trusted no one but myself. I eventually realized years later that I couldn't continue to allow my father's choices to affect MY choices, because we are different. Upon this realization I used that moment as fuel to become a different man instead of a carbon copy. Through prayer and study of the Word I've been able to change my mindset.

Now I'm a father and grandfather and I've completely changed the cycle that was set before me. In short, I'm present.

Apostle Thomas Evans Sr.

Founder/Pastor Dominion Worship Center
Charlotte, NC

Growing up I longed for male role model. My Dad left my Mom with three kids when I was about five years old. Because I had no man to show me what manhood was all about, I learned from the streets. Most of my life I battled trying to understand this thing called manhood. I had no one I felt close enough to who could take me under their wing and say let me show you how it's done.

The boy in me constantly battled with the man in me. Most of the time the boy won. I medicated the pain of life through sex. That was my comfort sin. If only someone had given me a manual after graduation that was a step by step tutorial on how a man was supposed to act. It didn't happen like that. Life soon taught me that I wasn't living at home with mama anymore and I needed to man up and do it quickly. Thank God for Jesus. Jesus became my instructor in masculinity. He taught me to love, to lead, and to provide as a man should. It didn't happen overnight though.

It took years of making mistakes before I half way started to understand what was required of me. Even today at 40 years old the boy wants to rear his head and respond to life as a 12 year old. Thank GOD for his grace and patience. Becoming a man and

MANHANDLED

"Hidden Code Words That Impact Men And The People That Love Them"

putting away childish things can be done. But it won't be done without a lot of stretching and sacrifice. If it were easy we would have more men showing up for life today instead of boys. We would have more families with Dads around leading the family through the maze of life. Now that I'm getting to the place where I'm understanding more about what it means to be a man, I'm able to help others on this journey. I understand now that masculinity is not in the amount of sex partners I have. It's not in the number of people I beat up. It's not in being loud and belligerent. It's about taking care of home. Loving my family. Avoiding the temptation to flirt with a woman who's not my wife. It's providing for my family in a honest way. It's about loving God, because without HIM, I'm nothing. I enjoy being a man today. Things I use to do in my ignorance is becoming a distant memory with every passing day. Now I have a son whom I can lead and direct past some of the pitfalls I fell into. We are on assignment here and I pray that you who are reading this find your transition from a boy to a man quicker than I did. We are in a day when men are gravely needed.

May God give you the wisdom and understanding of how to grow and succeed in your masculinity. We need you today!

Paul Bryant
KOG OUTREACH MINISTRIES.
CHARLOTTE, NC

AUTHOR OF " *IGNITING THE SPIRIT OF EVANGELISM***"**
and "*LADIES HERE'S WHY YOU KEEP CHOOSING THE WRONG GUY***"**
kogoutreachministries1@gmail.com

At 37 years of age, I suddenly found myself divorced and about to attempt this marriage thing all over again. With no real masculine guidance before or throughout my first marriage, it was easy to see why we crashed and burned. A major part of marriage is understanding what God said in His Word, about men being the head and both husband and wife need to understand this meaning. A man's leadership in marriage and in his home is not one of physical force, manipulation through violence, or some type of "caveman mentality" but rather through love, as taught by Christ. In the Bible, Ephesians 5:23 says – For the husband is the head of

MANHANDLED

"Hidden Code Words That Impact Men And The People That Love Them"

the wife, even as Christ is the head of the Church; and He is the savior of the body. Jesus Christ leads us in love. Today my marriage is great. I've learned to love, respect and share in what my wife is feeling as I lead, in a godly way. I'm still the man but with a different approach.

Pastor Carlton Whisonant

Pastor/President @ Mountain Be Removed Outreach Center (on Facebook)
Location: Pennsylvania

Professional: Chef 35+years, Caterer and The Healing Chef, can be found –Facebook, Twitter, LinkedIn, Instagram and Tsu. Web Address: cwwhisonant.wix.com/the-healing-chef

---

Passion in the Wrong Direction

Socially constructed, but made up of both socially-defined and biologically-created factors, distinct from the definition of the male biological sex. *Masculinity* is simply the transition from boyhood to manhood. The journey every male must take.

One of the greatest challenges for me with this transition was doing it without my biological father. Although other men in my family stepped up to ensure I wouldn't fail, that void was still very real. Masking the pain only resulted and manifested in wrong decision making. "Passion in the wrong direction" became my compass. It's what I call loving without boundaries. Anything you love abnormally becomes passion in the wrong direction. For me, it was loving me (being full of myself i.e. *pride*), my gifting, my talents, and multiple women at a time.

Anytime your output becomes more than your intake, your upkeep will become your downfall. I needed help because my attributes were swiftly developing into what had been absent in my life, my biological father. I needed deliverance, I needed to be healed. Although I had a relationship with God, I began to love other things more than I loved Him. I had to repent because I was taking on life without acknowledging the One who was always present focusing on what wasn't. It's an incontrovertible truth: ***transformation*** begins with loving your scars; not the "action of others" but the behavior of "self." When my relationship with God

MANHANDLED

"Hidden Code Words That Impact Men And The People That Love Them"

was restored, the relationship with my biological father was healed. God help me to understand that I needed to forgive. I needed to walk in forgiveness and extend grace so that I could reciprocate once needed. God healed me and now that healing is evident in my marriage, with my children and even the church I pastor.

Remember boys play with toys while real men build homes. "Except the Lord build the house, they labor in vain that build it:"- Ps.127 :1a

Apostle Corey Thompson, M. Div.

Power Center International, Atlanta, Ga
P.O. Box 896, Stockbridge, Ga 30281
678.787.0528

THE MAN I AM

From my childhood, many word curses were spoken over my life. Those curses harmed me and held me in a prison of limitations and handicaps.

"I thought you was going to be something. You ain't gonna' be nothing."

"You black."

"You ugly."

"You one nappy headed boy."

These words and many others warred against my soul injuring me for many years. I became hard and angry. When others would correct me I would retaliate by lashing out or withdrawing.

But Holy Spirit came in the right time and filled me. It was the beginning of my transformation. In 1992, I purchased a book. The Wonderful Spirit filled Life by Doctor Charles Stanley. I read that book as if I was a thirsty man drinking water after being in a desert. On December 31, 1992, I was filled with the Holy Spirit and my life was never the same.

Apostle Bernard Boulton. Watchman On Walls Apostolic Prophetic Fellowship.

Author of the Seventy: A Movement of Creativity in the Earth.

www.creativeawakenings.us

Bernard Boulton, Pastor of New Mine Creek Church http://WWW.FACEBOOK.COM/NEWMINECREEK Author of DO YOU WANNA BE MADE WHOLE? and JAKE AND ERIC in HOME AGAIN, STORIES OF RESTORED RELATIONSHIPS.

WWW.BERNARDBOULTON.COM

WWW.FACEBOOK.COM/BERNARD.BOULTON

HTTP://TWITTER.COM/IDEALWRITER

MANHANDLED

"Hidden Code Words That Impact Men And The People That Love Them"

Visit my blog at WWW.BERNARDBOULTON.BLOGSPOT.COM.

Sexually immoral is the man I was. I went from entertaining myself with pornographic materials to a habit of masturbation to a habitual sexual addiction that would lead to mental and physical consequences. I know what it's like to face the embarrassment of visiting the clinic, as well as the college infirmary. I know what it's like to be a "baby daddy." Child Support has been a thorn in my flesh for years. I know what it's like to travel up and down the road to have visits with my son. Then I would go through a drama filled marriage while fathering two children. All I can say is, "But God!" In spite of it all, Jesus has forgiven me of my sin. He has given me his peace that surpasses all understanding. He has fixed my marriage and blessed me to be a servant unto his glory, honor, and praise.

Lamont

I have always been a go getter in life since my youthful years and was able to accomplish much by the grace of God by having a positive thinking knowing that "Nothing is impossible with God". But a real challenge that I faced was being married for twenty plus years and didn't have a child to call my own, and still being called into ministry. The only thing that kept me going and not looking back or giving up was, the sure promise from God of a Male child. There is nothing that God says that He can't do, you only have to wait for it, even though it tarry. God has delivered on His promise, and today I am joyful father of a Son that I call my own. Just be patient in waiting. I decree over your life!

You are next in line! In Jesus mighty name! Amen.

Bishop Bennet Aboagye

Woodbridge, VA
Renew Life Worship Center

MANHANDLED

"Hidden Code Words That Impact Men And The People That Love Them"

One of the biggest things I had to face as being a man is when I went through my second divorce. I was doing okay after it but then it really began to break me down. When you go through things like that you begin to lose your identity. I was living with my friend and he is a Pastor of a church. We were both dealing with our issues and we were able to help each other out. But my heart was in serious pain and it made me question everything about my life. Pain will cause you to do things that you are not use to doing.

I felt like I did not know my identity anymore, I felt like I couldn't be loved. I discovered that men doubt themselves also, especially when they go through something as painful as a divorce. I got back up by asking God to help me every day. I began to focus on writing books and spending time with my kids.

No matter what you go through in your good times, bad times, good decisions, or bad decisions take God with you! One thing about an eagle is you see things differently than an ant.

Dr. Stewart McClain

Founder of Greater Revival Outreach Center
http://www.groccworldwide.com

One of the greatest struggles I've in countered in my masculinity has been fear! The fear of failure: is my best good enough? The fear of failing my children: is Daddy enough? Fear of loving again: can I really be trusted with what God has committed to my trust? I overcame fear because I began to be very honest with myself in all things. As I exercise being honest, yes exercise, because faith and honesty takes work, I came to the place where I was tired of me. I was tired of living the life of mediocrity. But as I embraced Gods trust in me that He had from the foundation of the world, I conquered my fears. How did I do it? "There is no fear in love; but perfect love casteth out fear: because fear hath torment. He that feareth is not made perfect in love." 1 John 4:18 KJV

Jacobby Debouvier: Songwriter, Music Publisher, Fashion Photographer, Author, Founder of the NAACP Black Men Rock Image Awards ; FB: Jacobby Debouvier Public Figure

MANHANDLED

"Hidden Code Words That Impact Men And The People That Love Them"

Several years back I was a young married minster full of zeal and passion. My wife, my GIFT is a true blessing from God. I met her in the 5th grade and she went from being my crush to my WIFE! Being a young minister full of zeal and passion I neglected my family for the sake of ministry. How stupid I was! To my surprise, I found out my gift of God(wife) had fallen out of love with me! I tried everything to make it better myself but nothing helped! It was when we sat with Pastor Jason, he totally blasted me for neglecting my wife and I how put my zeal and passion before her. That hurt! It was the lowest time in my life! Here is what he gave me that stuck with me and is the reason why my wife and I are deeply in love. As Men we are to LOVE her, Listen to her, Learn her, and Lead Her. Every time I have an opportunity to tell any young man who is about to get or is married I tell them to do those four things and I believe they will have a happy marriage!

Pastor Frank Lee
Faleejr@gmail.com

https://www.facebook.com/frank.a.lee.16

At the beginning of my career, I took a sales position to where I was the only minority in the entire organization . At first, due to my race, no one wanted to train or help me with anything. I felt alone. I spoke with my Dad about the situation and after going over some things he said, "So you're not going to quit... are you?" I understood what I had to do. I had to prove to myself and everyone that I could make it. I became very well liked within the company and communicated regularly with one of the owners.

My stand also led to other minorities being hired into the company. I was featured in commercials and given extra responsibilities. I had an extremely high referral rate from my customers and respected by peers. My father gave me what I needed to continue...A do not quit attitude!

Charles Davis

I AM MAN
(DR. OLIVER T. REID)

I am man, chiseled from earth's frame, held by the palms of God Himself. I am man, sculptured into an image that only mimic the portrait of God the Creator Himself. I am man, a byproduct of when God took a selfie. Then without hesitation, God placed me on top of the earth. He pulled me out of and commanded me to have dominion of all that was created beforehand.

I am man and my status has evolved and revolved since my existence, often I go missing, robbed from my identity, and left out of commission. I once was deemed the king of my family, now I have been renamed. I've been reduced to just a significant other, somebodies brother or just a baby daddy and a byproduct of when Harry met Sally.

I am man, left in the shadows of a world that can't spell my name even though God gave me the domain to its address. The caress of simplicity has distorted my definitions now when my name is called I answer at a lower position. Today I answer you when you call me boy. Now, how do I explain this to my son or to my unborn seeds that I no longer adhere to God's blueprints? See these modern day supplements left me high off the hangover from the intoxication from the lies of this current age.

I am man, full of countless volumes before my chapters were edited to mere indents on the pages of today's times. I am first not an excerpt to this blog you call evolution.

I am man. I stand erected without erection, worth more than just the potency of my seed to reproduce. Have you taken the time to search the shelves of the spin-off of God's creation? Can you see my produce beyond the penetration? Grasp this--my stock isn't contingent on the size of my Dow Jones. I'm totally bigger than that. Before the infection of outside subjections caused by the misdirection of truths appearing to be real. I desire to fill you but your belly is still full of the stuff that numbs you of my existence.

I was created to provide and administer protection and affection. Understand my queen use to love me for me. This was long ago. Light years before I traded in my dominion for rotten apples that altered our roles. You emerged as provider, I became receptor and

MANHANDLED

"Hidden Code Words That Impact Men And The People That Love Them"

we have never been the same. We fell helplessly in love with role reversal, without rehearsal. See we were never supposed to practice or act out of our characters, it was never in God's divine script.

I am man, far deeper than the muscles lying underneath the epidermis of my skin. Look closer and tap into the power buried under my structure. Can you restructure the way you see me?

I am man and my name is developer. I am called to build houses and not just be capped off by the limitations of simply paying house payments or rent. I am earth's foundation, the father of nations. I am man, understand the blueprints to God's plan. Can you hear me calling out from the noise of the mental music that plays the record of madness, echoing the tune of what you were told I am? I am the essences of God's compound when his thoughts collide with dust and earth. I am undeniably, undefinably Man.

DR. OLIVER T. REID

CONTENTS

	INTRODUCTION	xxxvii
1	Manhandled	1
2	Manipulation	7
3	Manifestation	20
4	Man Hood	27
5	Manhole	39
6	Manslayer	45
7	Many Mantraps	56
8	Man-less	69
	MY SON SHALL RISE AGAIN	74
	XMEN	85
	TONGUE TIED	87
	CONCLUSION	89

DR. OLIVER T. REID

MANHANDLED

"Hidden Code Words That Impact Men And The People That Love Them"

INTRODUCTION

It's no coincidence that even the greatest men are reduced to mere crumbs by the words they fail to comply or respond to. You can have a man of great stature be diminished by one word. The very essence of words are power and life. Words set a hidden stage under the feet of every man that ever walked on planet earth.

A word can hinder a man for his entire lifetime. Words propel men forward. One word given to a man can inspire him for a lifespan. Just a mere word changes the dynamics of the paths a man will take, let alone sentences or phrases. The supremacy of spoken words also paralyzes men, leaving them immobile. Why is it that these words have so much power? What gives words such a handle on men? I believe every single word in life has a code deeply embedded within them. These codes can't be confused with diction, tone, and language. You see, words are much more powerful than the way they sound or the accents that cover them.

The potency is in the seed of the word spoken. Every word has a code that locks a man in or out of something.

I like to call these Code Words. Code words press the spiritual, emotional, mental and physical accelerator of a man. On the other hand, there are code words that press the spiritual, emotional, mental and physical brakes in a man's life. Some code words simply shift a man into spiritual, emotional, mental and physical neutral. Hang on and trust that the next things I will share with you will be life transforming to say the least.

Let's look at this from the beginning of creation. God spoke before he formed man and he responded. When God made Adam he called him by name which carried an order, function, origin, and a purpose. In other words God gave Adam a domain that logged him directly into His frequency or divine coding. This happened way before God gave man a physical body. Genesis chapter 1:26-27. He told man to have dominion over everything he created first. God downloaded the domain address to man so that He could give him total access to the earth. Believe it or not, God completed the transfer to Adam by and through his spoken word. God himself

MANHANDLED

"Hidden Code Words That Impact Men And The People That Love Them"

was encrypting or placing a pattern of the plans and destiny for man inside of every word he said to him.

Man responded and started operating by God's spoken word. Adam reacted to the Code Words God spoke. Without hesitation Adam began to act out on the stage God had set with his words. He named all species one by one. When you name something you give it a function and order. Do you know that a dog can't be a deer simply because of the name Adam gave them? A bird can never be a lion solely because of the name? A man can never be a woman as a direct result of the label God gave her through Adam. Did you know that identity is established by the words men speak over something? The very word(s) a man speaks brings about identity.

Adam names his wife and gave her a role and function.

[21] So the Lord God caused a deep sleep to fall upon Adam; and while he slept, He took one of his ribs and closed up the flesh at that place. [22] And the rib which the Lord God had taken from the

man He made (fashioned, formed) into a woman, and He brought her *and* presented her to the man. [23] Then Adam said, "This is now bone of my bones, And flesh of my flesh; She shall be called Woman (Genesis 3:21-23 AMP)

The command of God's word transferred everything to Adam to fulfill his assignment. When God spoke the word it carries Adam to where He ordains Adam to go. It wasn't until the serpent spoke a new language or unauthorized code to Adam through Eve that caused man to be locked out from God.

In this book, my goal isn't to wow you with words but to show that every word a man encounters bares an imprint. I want to highlight the proven fact, that every spoken or written word a man comes into contact with has the potential to shape his identity in one way or another. As you read, I will uncover the reality that words possess both keys and locks, it's all in how you use them. My desire is that you will choose your words wisely. Words are both treasures and ammunition.

MANHANDLED

"Hidden Code Words That Impact Men And The People That Love Them"

If you're a man or woman who's ever asked yourself these following questions this is the book for you. Why do I keep locking myself in or out of the doors that are supposed to be locked or unlocked? Why is that I can't control myself? Why won't he or she listen to me? Why can't anyone get through to him? What happens when a man deals with man issues? Why are men all the same but different at the same time? Why can't I be the man I want to be? Why won't men fight fair? Why are the greatest strengths of men also their greatest weaknesses? Why are the words men speak or write so important?

My ultimate goal is to make you aware that every word or expression a man communicates leaves clues or patterns that will reveal who they are, where they've been, what they have endured, and the direction they are going. We need only to pay attention and words will lead us right to the core of a man.

I have spent some time researching code words that directly and indirectly affect every man on the planet. Evidence of these code words can be founded within Bible. Words that if you pay close attention to them, you will hear and synchronize yourself to the pulse of every man. These words have man written all over them and have manhandled men for countless generations. During this word study, we will examine them one by one.

My plan is to give you the codes that pick the door locks to men's hearts, minds, and spirits. I pray that after you read this book you'll hold the keys to improve relations, strength marriages, sustain families, dismantle generational curses, celebrate masculinity, empower fathers, uplift sons, and improve communication with men.

1. MANHANDLED

Manhandle (v.), mid-15c., "wield a tool," also, late 15c., "to attack (an enemy)," from man (n.) + handle (v.). Nautical meaning "to move by force of men" (without levers or tackle) is attested from 1834, and is the source of the slang meaning "to handle roughly" (1865). In the Bible the term often refers to shaking violently, to manhandle (literally, "shake someone to-and-fro"); intimidate, coerce (blackmail, extort), forcing someone to comply under threat (of being exposed, imprisoned, or put to death).

Men everywhere have been manhandled whether they know it or not. Some men won't admit that they've been forced to do things (physically, mentally, and spiritually) by words that they really don't or did not want to do. From little boys men are taught to take a licking and keep on ticking. Men are groomed to smile through pain and mask what they really feel. Many were told not to cry when they fell down. The vast majority of men were trained to respond differently than the way they feel.

Men have been intimidated by other men and women since time began. For example, a boy who was verbally or physically shaken to and fro by his mother or father figure, when he expressed his feelings and emotions growing up often suppresses his feelings. The male who had to do things by force often enters adulthood and forces others to do things against their will. It is important to note that a man that has been manhandled will manhandle others. A boy that was threatened, blackmailed, and imprisoned on the merry go round of life will definitely return the deeds dealt to him.

Manhandled men don't always reveal their wounds at first glance but if you stay around them long enough the side effects of the trauma they've experience will leak out. The results of manhandled men can be downright fatal and often cause a chain reaction. Let's take a look at manhandling in the scriptures.

MANHANDLED

"Hidden Code Words That Impact Men And The People That Love Them"

Manhandled

As Abram tricked Pharaoh into manhandling Sarai (Genesis 12.10-17), so Sarai would, in turn, persuade Abram to manhandle Hagar (Genesis 16:1-4). Later in the biblical narrative, a Pharaoh who had no recollection of Joseph would see the Children of Israel as a threat and legislate the manhandling of the entire people group (Exodus 1:11, Exodus 5:14).

Manhandling is contagious and can spread like wildfire. A man that is a byproduct of manhandling can pass it on from one generation to the next. There is a code you must break or deactivate in every man that has been mishandled. The code is awareness. Awareness of a matter will crack the code.

One should understand and locate the handle behind the man. Find what has handled him and you can retrace the path that's leads him to where his is now. Ask yourself these questions. What has a handle or strong hold on this man? If you find what or whom has mishandled the man in your life, you can discover the lever that triggers his actions, beliefs, emotions, and thought process. What is the source of his behavior? Be cautious not to get lost in the maze of his behaviors or actions.

Men that are manhandled or manhandling use words that: intimidate, bind, push or pull, and move others by force. A man that is manhandling someone is going to use his words and actions to force their agenda either directly or indirectly. During this time he is only mimicking what he has learned and feels will allow him to succeed in whatever he wants to accomplish. Again this a moment to pause and use awareness and understanding. This is not any easy task by any means but if your able to enter a new code word(s) at this time you can intervene.

Here are some words or intervention you can use to plant a different seed in the garden of a man's heart. Trying engaging in conversation and using these words below. Just don't speak these words but exude them by your behaviors and actions. Act out the words and watch the impact they have over time.

- ✓ Nurture

MANHANDLED

"Hidden Code Words That Impact Men And The People That Love Them"

- ✓ Foster
- ✓ Caress
- ✓ Cater
- ✓ Cherish
- ✓ Favor
- ✓ Gratify

The way in which you deal or handle a man that has been manhandled is key. You can't fight fire with fire or get into power struggles with this man. Use care and freedom to decode the code of manhandling. Provide an nurturing environment that fosters favor, and gratitude. Caress his ego and build relations that cater to the needs of his masculinity. Note that every man is different but each man needs to hear these words.

For example if a man is engaging in manhandling behavior or actions, simply provide a setting that allows him to be favored. You must be patient and possess the willingness to let the power of your words take root. This isn't an overnight process. Process makes perfect not the time of the process. Remember it is not your job to bear the ownership of the change that needs to take place in this man's life. You must run a gut check on yourself to see if you are truly committed to being a conduit of the change that you genuinely desire to occur in the life of a man. Take note that this isn't a license to stay in a verbal or physically abusive situation. This is simply a challenge to use your words wisely. Never try to manhandle a man that has endured manhandling, it is a battle where no one can win.

2. MANIPULATION

Manipulation (n.), c. 1730, a method of digging ore, from French manipulation, from manipule "handful" (a pharmacists' measure), from Latin manipulus "handful, sheaf, bundle," from manus "hand" (see manual) + root of plere "to fill" (see pleio-). Sense of "skillful handling of objects" is first recorded 1826; extended 1828 to "handling of persons" as well as objects. Strong's 3155. maten -- in vain, to no purpose. Accusative case of a derivative of the base of massaomai (through the idea of tentative manipulation, ie Unsuccessful search, or else of punishment); folly.

Manipulation is such a powerful word that has tied men in knots for ages. How can one word be used to control the masses? I've seen the greatest men fall prey to the hands of their manipulators. How is it that the smartest and brightest men get manipulated by another man who couldn't scratch the surface of their own mental, spiritual, and physical capacity.

The answer lies in the code of the word. Manipulation sells the recipient a handful of stolen or counterfeit goods. In other words, manipulation demands participation or the buying into of a thought or belief system. The man that was sold the falsehood that his worthless, unworthy, less fortunate, and useless will not only purchases the tickets of this falsehood, but acts it out on the stage of life. Manipulated men repeatedly punch the code through their actions and demand that those around them believe or buy into the untruth. Find a man bought by manipulation and you will soon discover that he wants to control or manage the thermostat of his environment. A man that is being manipulated has chosen to be a participant in the process of manipulation. Whether he knows it or not he has indirectly or directly played into the hands of manipulation.

The fact of the matter is a man that has been subject to manipulative behavior in his past will almost always drag it with him. Repeat after me: manipulation robs a man of his true God given purpose and paints a picture that he is doing just fine. A manipulated man always manipulates.

MANHANDLED

"Hidden Code Words That Impact Men And The People That Love Them"

The first man came face to face with manipulation in the Garden of Eden. Man was in a place of utopia until he bought the wolf tickets that the serpent (Satan) was selling.

The Fall of Man

Genesis 3 1 Now the serpent was more crafty (subtle, skilled in deceit) than any living creature of the field which the Lord God had made. And the serpent (Satan) said to the woman, "Can it really be that God has said, 'You shall not eat from any tree of the garden'?" 2 And the woman said to the serpent, "We may eat fruit from the trees of the garden, 3 except the fruit from the tree which is in the middle of the garden. God said, 'You shall not eat from it nor touch it, otherwise you will die.'" 4 But the serpent said to the woman, "You certainly will not die! 5 For God knows that on the day you eat from it your eyes will be opened [that is, you will have greater awareness], and you will be like God, knowing [the difference between] good and evil." 6 And when the woman saw that the tree was good for food, and that it was delightful to look at, and a tree to be desired in order to make one wise and insightful, she took some of its fruit and ate it; and she also gave some to her husband with her, and he ate. 7 Then the eyes of the two of them were opened [that is, their awareness increased], and they knew that they were naked; and they fastened fig leaves together and made themselves coverings.

This passage of scripture clearly illustrates the affect that manipulation had on the first man and woman. Adam is given a fruit that he knew about all along and had been commanded by God not to eat of it. Yet Adam eats and indulges. Why did he partake of the fruit of the forbidden? Remember the tree and the fruit was in Adam's garden all along and he had managed to refrain from it until the serpent spoke to his other half. See Satan released the code of manipulation in the ears of Eve. Then Eve partakes of the lie and offers the same untruth or distorted reality to her husband.

Recall from what I spoke of earlier, man responded to the words that was spoken over him by God. Man reacted to what I like to call the God code and began to fulfill God's manuscript in the

MANHANDLED

"Hidden Code Words That Impact Men And The People That Love Them"

earth. Man had never heard another voice or command by another before until Satan spoke the codes of manipulation. Take notice nothing happened immediately when Eve ate of the fruit but when Adam consumes the fruit it brought a dominion shift. Immediately Adam's and Eve's eyes(perspective and awareness) were opened and they began to be subject or bound by what God had given them dominion over. Satan knew if he could unveil the code of manipulation in a perfect world it could manhandle man's environment.

Dominion For Apples

The code that Satan used through the form of the serpent is still used today and is still in operation in unregenerate men's life today. I like to define this as the language of manipulation. Satan had distorted the truth and manipulated man into trading over his authority. It is imperative to know how Satan used manipulation to get man out of his position. Many biblical scholars debate over the fact that the fruit Adam and Eve consumed was today's apples (the word for sin and apple is the same in Greek.) but they all agree that it was a fruit of some sort. I'm going to use the concept of the apple to drive my next points home. Let's see how Satan uses the serpent to trick Adam into pawning in his dominion and God given authority for apples.

I. The first thing Satan uses the serpent to do was to talk to Adam's other half . In other words he wanted to see if he could present another perspective. The goal was to get Eve to see something different than her husband. Beware men Satan is still using this tactic today. Satan will love to use those things closest to us to manipulate us. Don't let the Serpent do it. When you hear a different language or set of instructions that are contrary to what God has commanded you to do don't buy into it. Men even the closest ones to you is not exempt from speaking a lie.

II. The second thing the Serpent did by means of manipulation was to divide and conquer. Satan spoke to Eve directly and didn't ever address Adam directly but issued him a fatal blow indirectly. Men must remember that Satan has no respect or reverence for authority figures. Beware of these codes that try to convenience you to avoid or usurp authority.

III. Thirdly, the Serpent offered Eve and Adam something they could have but couldn't afford. Satan offers the forbidden fruit. A key thing to keep in mind is that the apple or forbidden fruit was unguarded and right in the reach of man and woman. The power of your choice can be manipulated. Today time is no different. Men are still choosing apples over standing in dominion. Today, men would rather exchange their dominion for apple bottoms. Today's man would prefer consuming the flesh of the apple rather than maintain dominion over the entire garden. In society the masses of men's appetites aren't satisfied with the peace in their garden they seek to see what's behind the other tree.

Just like Adam, men today seek for one more slice of apple pie instead of being sustained by the provision already provided for them. Instead of reigning and ruling over their bodies and households they fall victim to the code words of manipulation and bite into the apple of role reversal. We must realize that's what happened when Eve provided the fruit to Adam and he took it, she (Eve) became the provider and he (Adam) became the receptor. Role reversal took place as result of manipulation the serpent placed in the garden. The code of manipulation is alive and still in activation. Now a days men have grown accustom to receiving instead of providing. Be aware of placing more value on things than the dominion you have already been given. Men, understand that it cost you to shrink or become less than who you are created to be. Never forget that no apple (**appealing, promised, potential, leading to exile**) is worth your place and right standing with God. Please don't bite the apple for instant gratification in exchange for prolonged isolation. These Apples of Opportunity come in all colors, shapes, flavors, and sizes but the constant is they all have a worm of deceit inside of them. Men beware these apples look amazingly beautiful on the outside but have a

MANHANDLED

"Hidden Code Words That Impact Men And The People That Love Them"

deadly aftertaste and a worm (worry, out of order, ruining, mandate) on the inside.

IV. Lastly, Satan didn't and could not take Adam's dominion. Satan knows his place no matter what he sounds or looks like. Therefore seek to know that our adversary Satan used manipulation to trick Adam to handing him his authority. In the same way Adam heard the command from God which stated that he couldn't eat the fruit of the tree, Satan heard it too. Key point men, Satan knows what God has commanded you to do and the function you are to carry out and he will always try to distort or decrease the value it. You must refuse to hand it over. Please don't fumble the ball on the field of life and hand your victory over to a defeated foe. Guard your authority by pleasing God with your choices. Never hand him (Satan) your rightful place. Don't let him stay in the garden of your life. Whatever ever you do don't reason with the serpent of manipulation.

> Remember, the Serpent doesn't have a right to speak in your garden.

Manipulation takes on many forms and seeks to control. When dealing with a man who is operating under the influence of manipulation you must recognize the code and deactivate it. Most importantly, one can't succumb to attempting to manipulate a man that is already exhibiting manipulative behaviors. It is a must that you not provide an atmosphere conducive to manipulation. When encountering a man that is being manipulative its vital to know it's not about the facts, because he will only see it from his filters. For instance, a man who is believing a lie about his life will begin to convince himself to believe it. If your primary focus is on proving him wrong by providing a list of facts, it may cause the man to increase manipulative behaviors.

The goal in this scenario should be to provide a man with the ability to choose a new filter or window to look out of. Changing the filters will increase the flow of truth and cut off manipulative behaviors over time. Prayer, patience and understanding are key

MANHANDLED

"Hidden Code Words That Impact Men And The People That Love Them"

but here are a list words you can use to help break the code of manipulation.

- ✓ Explain
- ✓ Solve
- ✓ Expound
- ✓ Leave alone
- ✓ Show
- ✓ Clarify
- ✓ Cleanse
- ✓ Refine
- ✓ Promote
- ✓ Illuminate

Provide a climate that promotes explanations without passing judgment. Give the man opportunities to explain. Be willing to clarify and allow him to bring clarity. Be cognizant that the man may need time to himself or time away to better assess the situation. Allow time for the man to find the correct filter to look through by creating windows of opportunity.

Illuminate truth without being intrusive, this can be done through highlighting when a man is speaking the truth about a situation. Take time to acknowledge the truth of the matter. Create an opportunity to cleanse the man. Wash him with kind words and provide room for error. Help the man problem solve if he ask for help. Please be attentive to when he ask for help both indirectly or directly. Your task is to provide the man with the right code: it isn't to be the code.

God will finish what you start. Allot time for the man that has manipulated you and others in the past to refine himself.

Trust me when I say it's easier said than done but it is possible if you allow yourself to be a bridge. Affirm your belief in him. Always evaluate yourself to see if you're using the right codes. Make sure you are looking at the situation through clear windows

MANHANDLED

"Hidden Code Words That Impact Men And The People That Love Them"

or filters. Don't allow yourself to be manipulated. Refuse to willingly participate in manipulation.

3. MANIFESTATION

Manifestation
To be clearly revealed unto man.

For the Scriptures say, "God has put all things under his authority." (Of course, when it says "all things are under his authority," that does not include God himself, who gave Christ his authority.) (1 Corinthians 15:27 NLT)

Manifestation is the translation of apokalupsis, "uncovering" (Romans 8:19, "the manifestation of the sons of God," the Revised Version (British and American) "revealing"); of phanerosis, "manifestation" (1 Corinthians 12:7 2 Corinthians 4:2).

Every man has been called by God to bring things into manifestation here on earth. Each man has been given a purpose and a manifesto by God Himself.

Every single man regardless of size, race, culture, disability, and background has been provided a platform or access code that will manifest things in their life. With that said, I can assure you that

MANHANDLED

"Hidden Code Words That Impact Men And The People That Love Them"

every man on earth will manifest or reveal something to the world in their lifetime.

Good, bad, or indifferent, men will leave their mark in this world. Some men manifest anger, rage, terror, and violence on the stages of their lives. Other men make evident their peace, problem solving ability, leadership, wisdom, and care on the canvass of the world. Never forget that it is innately inside of every man to bring something into manifestation. God put the need to manifest in the DNA of all men in the universe. Out of all the millions of sperm released during the time of conception, the man standing in front of you won. This man was a champion before he stepped out his mother's womb. Men are encoded with the ability to bring things from manifestation to demonstration.

For example, men begin to get upset or feel less than, when they are unable to show the evidence of what they've worked or toiled for. In other words, the frustrations of men derived from the perception of not being able to show proof of their labor reveals that they feel the call to fulfill.

Another example that men are called to bring things into manifestation is their desire to fix, repair, or build things. The code of manifestation prompts men to run to the rescue. This rescue code built into their DNA has gotten many men overtaken by manipulation. In conflict, the code of manifestation kicks into overdrive in men and often they just want to fix the problem instead of understanding where the problem is coming from. Despite being 'Clark Kent', men have the internal desire or passion to be Superman. Men just want to solve things by flying in to save the day.

Men feel the pressure to perform and leave their mark on this world. After all, men were called by God to walk out His manifesto. Men were placed on earth to be fruitful and multiple. However it is imperative for men to have balance in all of this. Furthermore, it is important to note that men need a safe place or conducive environment to manifest or bring things into manifestation. The atmosphere or platform must be filled with "can do's" instead of "can nots".

MANHANDLED

"Hidden Code Words That Impact Men And The People That Love Them"

Here are some keys factors that will to help induce manifestation in a man's life.

- ✓ A man will need an atmosphere filled with freedom and liberty. A man will have no problem exhibiting or expressing himself in a surrounding that celebrates and acknowledges him as a champion. Call a man a king or champion and he will respond as a king. Provide the atmosphere where he can reign and rule.
- ✓ Provide a stage or platform for him to be on display. Feed his ego (personality, character, self-image, self-worth, self-esteem, and identity).
- ✓ Take note, God Himself has an ego and man was created in his image and in his likeness.
- ✓ Understand the code of manifestation and become his biggest cheerleader, as he displays all of the talent and abilities God has already loaded him up with. Find a reason to celebrate or throw a party in honor of the man

regardless of the situation. Most of all be the man's audience. Every man whether they acknowledge it or not wants and has a desire to perform and be noticed on the stage of life and in the life of those he holds dear.

- ✓ Let the man leave his authentic mark or stamp on this world. Don't try to define his mark for him or erase it because it doesn't look identical to the next man. Please don't try to water down who and what he is in this world. Never forsake the fact that this man was created by God to leave his own individualized imprint on this planet. Be the envelope that provides a place for the man to place his stamp or postage on. Let the man in your life be able to provide validation and solidify his authority.

Below are some words that do not promote manifestation in men.

- ☒ Concealment – Don't try to foster a relationship that will advise the man to conceal his true identity. Avoid boxing the man into a mold or limit his potential.

MANHANDLED

"Hidden Code Words That Impact Men And The People That Love Them"

- ☒ Hiding – Refrain from advising the man to shrink or become less than who he is called to be. Do not facilitate dialogue and activities with or without the man that discourages him to expose his gifts, talents, and abilities. Exposure is key.

- ☒ Reality – Abstain from reminding the man of his current situation or the reality around him. Stay away from restricting the man to dream and speak his destiny into existence. Refuse to be a dream killer.

- ☒ Cover – Never attempt to camouflage the man's ability to manifest or bring notoriety to himself. Don't smother your champion.

- ☒ Don't throw things on top of the man's stage. Do not cover the man's platform.

- ☒ Obscurity – On no occasion do you endorse the man's insignificance. Refrain from making the man feel or appear small. Don't make the man look vague.

A man is crafted to manifest and pull things into manifestation. The man in your life was created to break barriers and open things that are sealed shut. If you allow your man to thrive in his God given habitat he will instinctively rise to the occasion and be what he was designed to be on planet earth. Make the man in your life feel like the super human being that he is, then watch him become noticeable, visible, evident, clear, and leave his patent on the world. Keep in mind, God has given every man a manifest destiny.

4. Manhood

Manhood,

early 13c., "state of being human," from man (n.) + -hood. Meanings "state of being an adult male," also "manliness," are from late 14c. Similar words in Old English were less explicitly masculine: manscipe "humanity, courtesy," literally "man-ship;" mennisclicnes "state of man, humanity, humaneness, human nature." The more "manly" word was werhad "male sex, virility, manhood".

We live in a world where a man is taught from adolescence not to cry. Today, parents tell their boys to man up, and command them to act like a man before they actually develop into one. I intensely feel that this is an injustice and deprives most men of their development and metamorphosis. What would happen if a lion was forced to be king of the jungle at a cub state? If this was to happen to the lion he would be devoured by the lesser species. What if a caterpillar was forced to be a butterfly before time? I believe the butterfly would fly awkwardly, simply because it has taken on a role prematurely. We can take away valuable lessons from observing the course of nature.

I feel very strongly that as a society we have pickpocketed the man of his developmental years by speeding up the process of manhood. A man's process suffers dearly if it is accelerated. Placing mature things on a boy's (*a male that lacks guidance*) shoulders can be fatal. For example, I wouldn't give my teenage son the keys to my car and sit in the passenger seat, expecting him to drive me around. The results would be devastating. First of all my 14 year old isn't authorized in the state in which I live to operate a motor vehicle. Secondly, he lacks the maturity to own the responsibility of driving my car. It would not be wise for me to allow my son to drive underage for many reasons. The same is true about allowing underage males to drive on the roads of manhood. They are unauthorized to set in a man's place. I firmly believe that many men have been given the keys or access to manhood before they were licensed to be one. It is so disheartening to see a boy trapped in a man's body. I call this the Man-child affect.

MANHANDLED

"Hidden Code Words That Impact Men And The People That Love Them"

Man-Child Affect

Man-child (n.), also man-child, "male child, male infant," c. 1400, from man (n.) + child.

The Man-Child Affect occurs when a young male is placed in the wrong position because he is viewed as the only option or alternative. The boy (*a male that lacks guidance or direction*) is given an access code to manhood that his mind, spirit, emotions, and body isn't prepared for. Imagine being thrown into the wilds of manhood when you're merely a boy who lacks the development to fill the roles of a man.

The Man-Child Affect can be seen any time you see an underage male in an identity crisis. When you see a teenager who speaks of raising his siblings and paying his Momma's bills, he is what I call a Man-child. Each time you over hear a young man speaking of the pressures to step up into a man's role he is a byproduct of the Man-child Affect. Young men who succumb to the Man- Child Affect feel trapped between two roles or two worlds.

They feel they must perform and do more with less. Although

these young males have the physical anatomy of a man, they lack the capacity to fulfill the role of a man, simply because they haven't matriculated into manhood. Just because the young man has a penis and a deep voice doesn't authorize him to be inducted into manhood. Many cultures have established a rite of passage because there is an innate understanding that guidance is needed for healthy transition.

There are many reasons young men are forced or put in position to take on the role of manhood prematurely. I'm going to discuss a few vital factors of why the Man-Child Affect occurs.

1. Due to the lack or shortage of men in the boy's environment or setting. Young men are recruited before they reach puberty to replace the man that has left their position vacant for whatever reason.

2. The filters or perceptions of those applying the pressure to the young male are distorted or skewed. Often time the parental figures view their young men as old enough to take on the position of a man. It can even be seen in referring to a boy as "my little man".

3. Feelings of hopelessness or abandonment are triggers

MANHANDLED

"Hidden Code Words That Impact Men And The People That Love Them"

that provoke young males into stepping up into a man's role. Many young males truly feel they are the only ones that can take care of themselves and their families. It truly breaks my heart as I travel the nations of the world to see boys standing in man postures. Often I ask them where is your father and the reply is, " I never knew him."

4. Following the leader. Men mimic what they see their father or mother doing. Boy's will conform to the pattern that is set before them. If they are told they are a man by those in authority they will do their best to adhere to those instructions.

The danger of a young man transforming into manhood prematurely is astounding.

When young men are exposed to manhood early they perpetuate the cycle, passing it on to the next generation. Each time a boy is put in a man's place it weakens the core of the family structure and deforms their growth and development process. How can a young man be a boy and the at same time, have to imitate the higher role?

Here are some things to help decode and dismantle the Man-Child Affect.

- ✓ Allow the young man to develop. Take on the role of a coach to move him forward. Don't trap the young man into worlds or roles. Advocate that the young man stays in the place of where he is now until he matures or graduates into manhood. There is nothing worse than a boy showing up later on in manhood.
- ✓ Don't apply unwarranted pressure to the young man's life. Refrain from discussing adult situations or circumstances with him prematurely. Premature engagement in the arena of adult hood can open up Pandora's box. Be careful what you expose the young man to. It will be hard to reverse the effects of the field once you have placed him on it.

MANHANDLED

"Hidden Code Words That Impact Men And The People That Love Them"

- ✓ Don't let him lead until he has been groomed to. Provide an environment that allows the young man to follow before he takes on a leadership role.
- ✓ If no man is present for the young man to set the pattern or expectation of manhood find one. Link the young man to mentors that have embraced manhood. There is nothing like a man who has embraced the journey of manhood; they make the best teachers.

Only a mature man can truly train a young man to be a mature man.

Man vs. Boy

Merriam-Webster

Below are some characteristics to examine that distinguish a man from a boy.

Man = An adult male human being with a particular occupation, responsibility, background, or nationality. One possessing in high degree the qualities considered distinctive of manhood.
Boy = A male child. A young man. An immature male <separate the men from the boys.

Manhood

Let's examine what the Bible states about manhood. A man must control his emotions and passions. Single or married, a real man subdues and controls his passions. He never abuses women or children, he protects them. He never touches or even entertains lecherous thoughts about a woman who is not his wife. He treats his wife with respect, dignity, and loving kindness. He takes the

MANHANDLED

"Hidden Code Words That Impact Men And The People That Love Them"

necessary precautions to always avoid pornographic images. He protects the virginity and innocence of all single women, especially his daughters. He's a man with a heart after God, not entirely unlike the best traits of King David.

A man must provide for his own family. First Timothy 5:8 says, "But if anyone does not provide for his own, and especially for those of his household, he has denied the faith and is worse than an unbeliever." When a man neglects to work and provide for his family, he cannot avoid a sense of shame and worthlessness. A lazy man creates insecurity in his wife and in his children. Every man also needs to provide for his family's emotional and spiritual needs. A father should train his children and prepare them to become responsible adults who know how to successfully negotiate their way through life.

A man protects his family. Being a protector calls for more than ensuring physical safety. Proverbs 4:10–15 describes a father who protects his son by passing on wisdom, helping him build godly character, and teaching him to reject the lies and temptations of the world.

This father protects not only his son but the generations to follow as the wisdom he shares gets passed on. He leaves a godly legacy.

A man serves and leads his family. While the Apostle Paul tells us in Ephesians 5:23 that "the husband is the head of the wife," he quickly puts to rest any notions that this leadership allows for self-serving male dictatorship. He completes the sentence with, "as Christ also is the head of the church." The passage goes on to say that husbands should love their wives "just as Christ also loved the church and gave Himself up for her" (Ephesians 5:25). This paints a picture of leadership contrary to how politicians view leadership. A man is called to be a servant-leader and to take responsibility for his wife and children. A husband must put the family's needs ahead of his own. He is called to demonstrate God's selfless and sacrificial love (1 Corinthians 13:4-7).

A man, by design, follows God's Scriptural plan for true masculinity. Micah 6:8 says, "He has told you, O man, what is good; and what does the Lord require of you but to do justice, to

MANHANDLED

"Hidden Code Words That Impact Men And The People That Love Them"

love kindness, and to walk humbly with your God?" The core of a man's life should be his steadfast and intimate relationship with God.

The man who walks humbly with God is provoked and empowered to step up and tackle the difficult responsibilities life will send his way.

Man In The Mirror

Manhood is a great place to be. Every man must take the time to look at himself in his own mirror. Notice I stated a man must look at his own reflection directly from his own mirror. The reason I recommend that men look at themselves is to avoid the urge to measure or equate themselves by the standard of the man next door. It is a must that all men run a gut check on themselves before someone else cast the ballot of their opinions of his manhood. When you take a look in the mirror men, ask yourself these hard questions. Am I being honest about my past, present, and future? Am I a man-child? Am I secure in my manhood? Why or why not? What defines me as a man? Who defines me as a man? What do I desire to accomplish as a man? Please don't take the easy way out and skip the opportunity to be real with yourself.

A man that embraces their manhood has the opportunity to shape his generation. The man who endures the transitioning from a boy to a man can be a monument in the earth for other young men to follow. Below are some words that demote the value of manhood of a man.

- ☒ Cowardice- Don't promote faintheartedness.
- ☒ Fear- Don't promote fear as to it relates to manhood.
- ☒ Timidity- Don't shy away from embracing manhood. Refuse to be bashful about who you are.
- ☒ Weakness- Embrace the weaknesses of manhood rather than avoiding them.
- ☒ Irresolution- Don't dwell in the valley of decision debating over your manhood. Men beware of falling into manholes.

MANHANDLED

"Hidden Code Words That Impact Men And The People That Love Them"

5. MANHOLE

Manhole, also man-hole, "hole through which a person may pass," 1793, from man (n.) + hole (n.). Manhole, n. a covered opening in a floor, pavement, sewer, etc. for workmen to gain access. A hole through which one may go especially to gain access to an underground or enclosed structure.

(Oxford Dictionary)

If you're like me, I grew up in the inner city. Daily, during my commute, I would walk or ride my bike by manholes and really didn't pay attention to them. Manholes became part of the scenery or pavement in the urban projects in which I lived.

It wasn't until one day I had a personal encounter with a manhole that I gained a newfound respect for them. One day when I was fourteen years old, I was on my way to my summer job at a nearby elementary school.

That day was just like all of the other days that I'd ridden my bike to work, accept there was a steady drizzle on the streets. Like most teenagers I didn't pay attention to the road conditions; in fact, I started to accelerate my speed in order to get out of the rain. Without a moments pause, the front tire of my ten-speed bike collided with a drain cover of a manhole. Needless to say I was dislodged from my bike, flipped several feet in the air, and finally slid head first to a complete stop several yards away. I still have the scars from this accident until this day.

Battered and bruised, I could only ponder over the fact that I'd become so familiar with the manhole being in place that I failed to take precautions. Let's just say that I never forgot the message behind the manhole. Have you ever gotten too accustomed to something dangerous in your life because it has blended into the scenery? Do you know every man has holes that camouflage themselves into the landscape of their day to day lives? Are you aware that most men don't even realize that the manholes in their lives have derailed them for years?

MANHANDLED

"Hidden Code Words That Impact Men And The People That Love Them"

Manholes are so encoded in the internal hardware of men that they don't see them until it smacks them in the face. Manholes are built to gives access to an enclosed area. Manholes allow things (***pain, rejection, fear, molestation, rage, anger, insecurities***) to drain down in and settle in the sewers of man's life. It is very important to look beneath surface of a man. You can't just look at a man at face value.

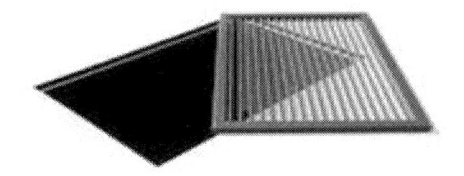

Manholes Lead To Man Caves

Contrary to popular beliefs and opinions, men wrestle with internal struggles just as much as women do. A man's heart leaks issues that might not readily show up in his external persona.

Trust me there may not be any tears shed from the eyes of the man that's stuck in the manholes of his life. Please don't be deceived. It could be that the man that doesn't show his emotions has grown accustom to the trauma he is enduring.

For example, a man that has endured severe rejection since his conception often elects to isolate himself from the situation. The man backs himself into a cave of suppression as a defense mechanism to shield himself from the constant pain of rejection. Manholes in men's lives have the potential to pin their backs against the wall. Some men would rather hide in the cave than fight to change their environments. Other men feel that it takes more effort to heal or recover than to dwell in the sewer of their situations. Beware of a man that refuses to come out of the basement or man cave. A man that is physically, emotionally, spiritually, and mentally detached from his environment is dealing with manholes. These manholes or small cracks can't be overlooked or swept under a rug. You can't afford to ignore the code.

MANHANDLED

"Hidden Code Words That Impact Men And The People That Love Them"

Explore these code words to seal the manholes and pull men out of man caves.

- ✓ Entryway – It is imperative that you explore and research the entryways that have impacted the man's life. Look for the doors that has exposed the wounds of the man. Retrace the entryways and you will begin to discover where the man holes and man caves are.
- ✓ Crack – Pay attention to the small things that is leaking in the man's life. Be attentive to the discreet changes. Tiny cracks lead to gaping holes within a man's heart. Seal the small cracks with love, affirmation, and understanding. Remember small foxes spoil the vine. Search for small clues that has crept into the crevasses of a man's life. Look for the small things that carry big impact in a man's environment.
- ✓ Breach – Find the opening to the issue that is plaguing the man. Seek to locate the root of the matter the man faces.

Catch what is coming out of the man's mouth. Search for the rupture that is causing the man to pull away. Discern the disconnect between what the man says and what he does.

- ✓ Doorway – Distinguish where the doorway to the man's issue(s) lie. Locate the entranceway and find a way to walk through it. Ask questions about the man's past and listen to what he tells you. Shut the door to the triggers that lead to the manholes.

- ✓ Vent –Allow the man to vent in a non-judgmental environment. Be quick to listen and slow to speak. Close the vent off to negativity or false accusation about the man's situation or circumstances.

Men are to be the gatekeepers. Jesus Christ is the ultimate door.
"I am the door: by me if any man enter in, he shall be saved, and shall go in and out, and find pasture." (John 10:9)

6. MANSLAYER

Manslayer (n.), manslayer in the Bible Expand. One who was guilty of accidental homicide, and was entitled to flee to a city of refuge (Num. 35:6, 12, 22, 23), his compulsory residence in which terminated with the death of the high priest. (See CITY OF REFUGE.)

Smith's Bible Dictionary

Manslayer one who kills another unintentionally, and is thus distinguished from a murderer, who kills with malice aforethought. The cases of manslaughter mentioned in Scripture appear to be a sufficient indication of the intention of the lawgiver.

Death by a blow in a sudden quarrel. (Numbers 35:22)

Death by a stone or missile thrown at random. (Numbers 35:22,23)

By the blade of an axe flying from its handle. (19:5)

In all these and the like cases, the manslayer was allowed to retire to a city of refuge. A thief overtaken at night in the act of stealing might lawfully be put to death, but if the sun had risen, killing him was to be regarded as murder. (Exodus 22:2,8)

Don't Let Cain Kill Your Abel

You maybe be familiar with the infamous story in the bible that speaks about Cain and Abel. The story give an account of the two offspring of Adam and Eve.

Genesis 4 Now the man Adam knew Eve as his wife, and she conceived and gave birth to Cain, and she said, "I have obtained a man (baby boy, son) with *the help of* the Lord." [2] And [later] she gave birth to his brother Abel. Now Abel kept the flocks [of sheep and goats], but Cain cultivated the ground. [3] And in the course of time Cain brought to the Lord an offering of the fruit of the ground. [4] But Abel brought [an offering of] the [finest] firstborn of his flock and the fat portions. And the Lord had respect (regard) for Abel and for his offering; [5] but for Cain and his offering He had no respect. So Cain became extremely angry (indignant), and he

MANHANDLED

"Hidden Code Words That Impact Men And The People That Love Them"

looked annoyed *and* hostile. ⁶ And the Lord said to Cain, "Why are you so angry? And why do you look annoyed? ⁷ If you do well [believing Me and doing what is acceptable and pleasing to Me], will you not be accepted? And if you do not do well [but ignore My instruction], sin crouches at your door; its desire is for you [to overpower you], but you must master it." ⁸ Cain talked with Abel his brother [about what God had said]. And when they were [alone, working] in the field, Cain attacked Abel his brother and killed him. ~ Genesis 4:1-8 Amplified Bible (AMP)

This scripture clearly illustrates the response of two men to the same commandment God gave. It is totally mind blowing that two men can hear the same instruction(s) and respond differently. Cain and Abel were both commanded by God to bring a specific offering. Cain worked the field and brought God an average wage for an honest day of work. On the other hand, Abel presents God with the first or top of the line of all of his work.

Abel brings God the first fruit of his labor, while Cain just gives

God fruit. Cain was stuck on average meanwhile Abel was determined to break the back of mediocrity.

Cain got so angry and vengeful that he kills his brother Abel, shedding innocent blood. The first murder was birthed out of jealousy and anger over another man's gift to God. Take a few seconds to let that sink in. Cain kills Abel because of the gift he failed to bring to God. Abel is murdered because of the gift he brought to God. Cain takes on the role of a manslayer and Abel was forced to fulfill the role as the slain.

I use to often ponder over how two men can grow up in the same house, live under the same set of rules, go to the same church, work at the same exact place, and end up opposite of each other.

See I've come to the realization that every man has both a Cain and Abel growing inside of them. Believe it or not, each and every man has something good and something bad both growing internally. Each man has something(s) in his life he is slaying or giving life to.

A man who has great potential to do good things while at the same time he has the potential to do the wrong thing; it is locked up

MANHANDLED

"Hidden Code Words That Impact Men And The People That Love Them"

inside of him and is manifest through his decision making. The same hands of a man that brings life or cultivates something, can also damage and destroy it within the same breath. The same identical man that can build and construct an elaborate building can in turn choose to destroy it without a moment's notice. I hope you see the point. I've read stories where the same father who played a role in a child coming into the existence of the world, snatches the very life from them in the heat of anger or rage. A man can kill the thing he loves and live to regret it for the rest of his life. This is not an easy thing to understand and often baffles the masses. A man can speak life to something and a benediction to the exact thing within the next word that proceeds out of his mouth.

I have eye witnessed a man be a savior and a slayer at the same time. Contrary to popular opinion, every man has the potential to do this. Every man has the impending ability to become a slayer. Let's look at this in a broader sense.

You have some men who will self-sabotage their own dreams, ambitions, goals, future and legacy. Not because these men aren't passionate about their goals or legacy; it's not because they don't care. It is not even because they don't love life; it is because they simply feed the Slayer within them. It has been said that inside of every man there is a wolf and lamb. The one you feed the most will emerge as dominant. If you look closely, you can see this in your everyday life, there are times when you want to do something wrong even though you are morally good.

It is imperative to remember this next sentence. All men have the potential to kill. What the man decides to destroy, slay, kill or murder bares the weight of importance in his life. It is bad for a man to kill the innocent or annihilate those who cannot defend themselves. It is a harsh thing to self-sabotage or destroy your potential or the potential of others.

On the other hand it is outstanding for a man to kill anything (not in the literal sense) that opposes his potential or destiny. For instance, it is commendable for a man to cut off distractions, to rid himself of those things that hinder him from moving forward. It is

MANHANDLED

"Hidden Code Words That Impact Men And The People That Love Them"

creditable for a man to die for his country or to give up his life for what he believes in, to give up his life for his freedom. Jesus said no greater love have a man than laying down his life for his friends. It is considered honorable by most for a man to kill all those that stand in his way of the security and safety of his family. The Bible states in the book of Ecclesiastes 3:3 that to everything there is a season there is a time to kill. To drive this point home let's take a deeper look at some simple things Cain could have done to get back in right standing with God and change the outcome of his situation.

1. Cain could have a simply brought God what he wanted.
2. Cain could have apologized to God and repented of his ways.
3. Cain could have mimicked what his brother Abel was doing. Cain could have learned a lesson from Abele's example.

I want to show you the code words that will allow men to understand how to deal with both Cain and Abel in their lives.

- ☒ Assassin – Beware of the men that lay in wait to kill or assassinate a person, place, dream, or idea. A man that exhibits the behaviors of an assassin is feeding the spirit of Cain in his life. Men who are assassins often dispatch negative behaviors into the atmosphere.

- ☒ Butcher – These are men that display destructive behaviors. They are the men that thrive on tearing things apart. These are the men that raise Cain in their lives and those around them.

- ☒ Criminal – These are the men that get a kick out of breaking the law. This is the man that plots ways to connive their counterparts. These are the men that attempt to illegitimately gain more with less. They scheme and swindle without a conscience.

- ☒ Cutthroat – Men that don't attempt to mask their intent for destruction. This man openly reveals or exposes Cain like characteristics. These men are callous and numb to the results or consequences of their actions.

MANHANDLED

"Hidden Code Words That Impact Men And The People That Love Them"

- ☒ Executioner – This is a man who places himself in authority to carry out the death sentence to another. The spirit of Cain is alive on the inside of this man waiting for the opportunity to slay.

- ☒ Hit-and-Run – This is a man who is always on the move after he strikes someone. A man that hits and runs is operating with the same spirit as Cain did. These men also bare the curse of their reckless behavior just like Cain. They are wanderers who find a home but no peace.

[9] Then the Lord said to Cain, "Where is Abel your brother?" And he [lied and] said, "I do not know. Am I my brother's keeper?" [10] The Lord said, "What have you done? The voice of your brother's [innocent] blood is crying out to Me from the ground [for justice]. [11] And now you are cursed from the ground, which has opened its mouth to receive your brother's [shed] blood from your hand. [12] When you cultivate the ground, it shall no longer yield its strength [it will resist producing good crops] for

you; you shall be a fugitive and a vagabond [roaming aimlessly] on the earth [in perpetual exile without a home, a degraded outcast]." Genesis 4

- ☒ Triggerman –These are the men who kill others from a distance through their words or physical actions. These men usually work with likeminded men who possess the same mentality.

Repeat this once more, there is an Abel and Cain inside of every man. Which one are you willing to sacrifice? Here are some codes to help bring out the Abel characteristics in you.

- ✓ Speak Life – The power to live is in your mouth and no Cain can destroy you. Notice that Abel's blood cried out from the ground long after he was murdered by Cain. [10] The Lord said, "What have you done? The voice of your brother's [innocent] blood is crying out to Me from the ground [for justice]. What you do in life will eternally echo and keep God fixated on you long after you're gone.
- ✓ Please God With Your Sacrifice – Mimic Abel and bring

God what he wants. Give God your best in life. Become the sacrifice that God is pleased with.

- ✓ Don't Kill Your Brother! – Do not become jealous or be envious of what your brother is bringing to God. Men stay out of your brothers field.
- ✓ Kill the Right Thing – Notice that Abel killed the first fruit of his livestock in order to present God with the very best of what he had been blessed with. Whatever you do please don't kill your brother! Don't be afraid to sacrifice your very best to please God. Be the man that brings God the best gift.
- ✓ Be Willing to Die For The Right Cause – Abel was a man of sacrifice therefore he became a sacrifice for doing good.

7. MANY MANTRAPS

Many Old English monig, manig "many, many a, much," from Proto-Germanic *managaz (cognates: Old Saxon manag, Swedish mången, Old Frisian manich, Dutch menig, Old High German manag, German manch, Gothic manags), from PIE *menegh- "copious" (cognates: Old Church Slavonic munogu "much, many," Old Irish menicc, Welsh mynych "frequent," Old Irish magham "gift").

Mantrap (n.)
A trap, net, web, or dangerous entrapment for a man. A seductress. A beguiling or ungodly woman.

"Fearing people is a dangerous trap, but trusting the LORD means safety." (Proverbs 29:25 NLT)

"The man who visits her is doomed. He will never reach the paths of life." (Proverbs 2:19 NLT)

Unfortunately men live in a world of many. There are a surplus of options out there; many opportunities to fall into the snares of their own lust or selfish desires. Since the beginning of time men have desired more than they could handle and in the present day, the vast majority of men still thirst for more, despite being full to capacity. Some men want more for greed, others to quench their thirst for power or prestige. Whatever the reason, men have always fed the addiction to not only have their cups full, but to the overflow.

What is it that makes a man making six figures steal the petty cash from his boss's office? What causes a man that's married to the most beautiful woman in the city to betray his wife's trust for Ugly Betty? Why is it that a man can feel death kicking in his gut but still attend the party that takes his life? Why does a man eat himself to death when he is clearly stuffed to capacity? Where does a man get off wandering from place to place in search of conquering the next opportunity? The only answer I can come up with is too many options. There is simply too many, way too many alternatives for a man to choose from. The world is loaded with mantraps.

Men, beware. Mantraps are everywhere. Mantraps come in all shapes, sizes, smells, flavors, places, things, colors, cultures, and sounds. The common denominator that leads men to longing or wanting more is the cheese (***code(s), hidden, easily, entering, seduction, entrance***) piled on top of the mantrap. It is the cheese or bait that lowers men to their down fall. One must realize that bait is always something you would risk your life for. Men, if you're not willing to take the risk of possibility losing it all, it's not a temptation for you. If the mere smell of it sends chills down your spine every time you ponder over it and you desire to taste it after you have just eaten, it is the type of cheese you like. The bait (***believing, attitude, it's, temporary***) always leads men back to the mantrap. Men keep falling into the traps because they feel as though the trap was a temporary problem.

Let's examine what Mantraps are and how men fall into them. Mantraps are snares that cause a man to trespass against himself.

In other words, Mantraps are snares that a man willfully or unwillingly walks into that causes him detriment.

[16] For all that is in the world—the lust of the flesh [craving for

MANHANDLED

"Hidden Code Words That Impact Men And The People That Love Them"

sensual gratification] and the lust of the eyes [greedy longings of the mind] and the pride of life [assurance in one's own resources or in the stability of earthly things]—these do not come from the Father but are from the world [itself].

(1 John 2:16 Amplified Bible)

This scripture text undoubtedly reveals what mantraps are made of. See the code words that are at the core of all mantraps below.

- ☒ Lust of the Flesh – Mantraps pull or lure a man in by his own lust or desires. Men are trapped by what they are hungry for. Hungry men eat. In the bible **(Genesis 27)** Jacob was able to coerce his brother Esau into selling his own birthright or inheritance because of his hunger. A man's flesh is his greatest enemy. The 'inner me" of a man often called his soul (emotions, will, and intellect) is a constant battleground.

It is like a man shadow boxing against himself. No matter

how hard the man swings or punches, he can't outbox his own shadow because his reflection moves with him. Man is comprised or made up of three parts : Spirit, Soul, and Body. It is impossible to separate the three and they are identical to his shadow. For the sake of time I would like to focus on the soul of a man. The soul operates like a blank internal hard drive; whatever is saved to it will go with him. For instance, if a man has an impure desire saved or embedded in his soul that goes undetected or unrooted, it will play on repeat until it ensnares him . In simpler terms, what is on the inside of a man's fleshly desires will leak out on to the pages of his life.

☒ Lust of the Eyes – What a man sees will lead him right into the vices of Mantraps. Men are visual: we see, then we act. Men see and ask questions later. Men are often bound by their own perceptions. A man will set his sights on what he wants and pounce on it without assessing the consequences of his actions. Notice the lust of the eye is more than just wanting what you see. When a man lusts from his eyes he craves, yearns for, hungers after, and desires what he sees. The lust of a man's eyes will cause him to lunge headfirst into a Mantrap. [27] "You have heard that it was said, 'You shall not commit adultery'; [28] but I say to you that everyone who [so much as] looks at a woman with lust for her has already committed adultery with her in his heart. **Matthew 5:27-28 Amplified Bible (AMP)** Paraphrasing, Jesus said it best when he says that a man's eyes are just as harmful as his hands. What he lays hold to with his eyes can damage his soul long before his hands follow. Every man has an eye gate or entry way that leads to the field of his soul, spirit, and body. Find where or what a man is watching and be certain the rest of him will follow.

☒ Pride of Life – Men take pride in life some more than others. A man plans out his life and holds it close to his heart. By nature men are competitive, some more than others. From the sandbox, a little boy fights to make the biggest sandcastle and when he turns into a man he strives to build his house bigger than the men around him. Men parade around, boasting about the cars they drive, the positions they hold, and the amount of material possessions they have acquired. Men equate their substance with stuff. A man measures his status in life by what he has obtained and what he feels he has the potential to obtain. Some men display their competitive nature, while others do their best to conceal it. Some men are passive, yet others are aggressive but they all deal with the pride of life. The pride of life Mantraps men because they often pawn their integrity for stuff that they feel will validate them. Men fall victim to the Mantraps and often sell their soul for material possessions. Many men forfeit their families for successful careers and campaign their lives away in the name of their pride.

A lot of men auction off their legacy for their own agendas. We must avoid the Mantrap of pride at all costs.

MANHANDLED

"Hidden Code Words That Impact Men And The People That Love Them"

Many Options

Too many men collapse to the Mantrap of options. There are options all around men in this world. Men live in a world where juggling a mistress, side-chick, and the occasional one night stand is celebrated as notches on his belt and proven masculinity. Nowadays men have a pool of woman to dive into. A lot of men lay entangled by the surplus of the variety provided by the opposite sex, until they get lost in the assembly line. Men are drunken by the concoction of consuming to many (women) flavors at once.

4 And in that day seven women will take hold of one man, saying, "We will eat our own food and wear [and provide] our own clothes; only let us be called by your name; take away our shame [of being unmarried]." **Isaiah 4:1 Amplified Bible (AMP)**

Today men have more than one Eve to choose from meaning they often select the decoy to wed.

Men are seduced to the pit of Mantraps every day, as they suit up in tuxedos and walk down the aisle with another man's wife. Now they consummate inside of a Mantrap. Undisclosed to the man involved, he chooses a wife from all of the alternatives he has been provided through his own lustful desires. Often men gamble away the queen God has for them in exchange for milk and cookies. Blinded by options, men overlook their soul mate due to what has occupied their souls. God doesn't have the symptoms of bipolar or schizophrenia. God still intends for a man to have one option for a wife not many.

He Men With He Weaknesses

I have learned through much trial and tribulation that men ultimately don't have a woman, money, sex, power, success, fear, and addiction issue. Men have a god(s) issue. Men tend to fall into Mantraps because they want to play the role of God .

Since the beginning of time man has tried to do things without the ultimate consent of God. Men through the ages have attempted to work their way(s) around God, while somehow hoping to retrieve God's favor and provision. I call this the He Weakness. When men have an identity crisis because they try to assume the role of God either indirectly or directly. Men who try to minus God (or

MANHANDLED

"Hidden Code Words That Impact Men And The People That Love Them"

leave God out) experience He weaknesses. When a man stops being God's image or a He (God's) man, he attempts to be **T**he **M**an. The man absent from God begins to take on the full responsibility for his own life.

He (God's Man)becomes **T**he **M**an and takes on the responsibility for his marriage, house, car, family, relationship, job, and complete wellbeing. A man walking absent from God is a recipe for disaster to say the least. Prime example, when Adam takes the responsibility to eat of the tree God forbid him to eat from He (God's Man) became **T**he **M**an. As a direct result of Adam's life was reduced to bearing the responsibility of his own fate.

Mantraps - an illegal trap set to catch poachers or trespassers on private land, usually in the form of a metal device that snaps shut onto somebody's leg. A dangerous place, as an open hatch, into which one may fall.

Code words to counteract Mantraps

- ✓ (Aid) Disarm the Trap – Provide help and assistance to help the man come out of the Mantrap. Remember it's not your ultimate job to free the man that's ensnared but to be instrumental in disarming the code. Declare words of freedom over the man. The worse thing you can do to a man that is captured by a Mantrap is to press him down further.

- ✓ (Honor) Free the King, Trap the Wolf – Your task is to bring honor to the man and view him as a king despite the fact that he is caught inside of the Mantrap. See the man's kingship, not the mantrap he's in.

- ✓ (Honor, con't.) Releasing honor on a man breaks the cycle of dishonor. Honor wins over dishonor any day. Trap the wolf by starving it. Take the focus off the negativity that is growling or influencing the man. Don't feed the wolf with words of affirmation. Don't affirm the root cause of the crisis

.

MANHANDLED

"Hidden Code Words That Impact Men And The People That Love Them"

- ✓ (Release) Keys for Locks – Advocate for release. Again it is not your job to rescue the man found inside of the trap but you can play a key role in releasing the locks. Speak words to the man that uplifts and unlocks opportunities for change. Offer the man key solutions to problems, not problems that lockout solutions.

- ✓ (Openness) It's Not About You – Remain open to the man and don't shut down. See the trap not the man. Don't take the Mantrap personal! Don't make the trap about you! Use the grace code on your man by multiplying room for error to him.

- ✓ Don't Be A Trapper – A man inside of a Mantrap doesn't need to be restrained. Don't add fuel to the fire or fortify the trap that the man is in! Don't magnify the trap over the man!

- ✓ Bread for Cheese – Give the man in the Mantrap bread (**b**elief, **r**efuge, **e**mpathy, **a**ffirmation, **d**ominion) instead of cheese (**c**ode(s), **h**idden, **e**asily, **e**ntering, **s**eduction, *entrance*). Give the man positive and sincere words of encouragement and healing. Proclaim the Can Message and eliminate the Can't Note.

- ✓ Honesty – Speak truth and honesty over a man encountering a Mantrap. Give the man opportunities to be honest in a non-threatening environment.
- ✓ Blessing – Speak and declare blessings over the man in the Mantrap. Proclaim validation over the man inside of the pit. Let the man know that blessing over the man's life is larger than the trap he is in. Paint a realistic picture of hope for the man.

8. Man-Less

Man-less (adj.), Destitute of men. Unmanly; inhuman.

Naomi returns to Bethlehem man-less and destitute, and renames herself "bitter-woman.

"And she said unto them, Call me not Naomi, call me Mara: for the Almighty hath dealt very bitterly with me." (Ruth 1:20)

We live in a day and age where being a man isn't popular. Now a days the emasculation and feminization of men is running rampant across the world. It is almost a bad word in some places to say that you are a man. Even the males only bathroom signs are being renovated and relabeled unisex. More and more society is finding a means to replace or substitute the defining characteristics that define men as a whole. In many instances men are no longer valued or revered.

Patriarchal society is being cursed and the "goddess" culture is on the rise. In a lot of cases men are being mentally, emotionally, and spiritually castrated. Men are now given a ticket to wait in line to purchase a watered down or generic form of masculinity. Instead of being the head of the home, church, and family, most men are now being told by the mainstream to tuck their headship between their legs. Mass media plays the images of the new man upon the big screens of our culture displaying the infomercials of a new age man, one who is seen as lazy, domineering, disinterested in his role and eventually useless to the family structure. The man is being reduced to a role that is currently being rolled so far away that it's in danger of becoming extinct. Our societies are pushing the pill of encapsulated men down the throats of this generation and the next, to the chant of men don't matter.

It's becoming hard to stand as a man in a culture that promotes men as less than or equal to lower level status quo. Our men are being told by the legal system that basically all we need from you is the potency of your seed, your fatherhood is no longer required. The Government is happy to take the place of Fathers. Child support legislation has given a hall pass to men and demanded that

MANHANDLED

"Hidden Code Words That Impact Men And The People That Love Them"

they give their offspring rations instead of years. Women everywhere have bought into the lie that they can be the male and the female to their children. After all these women have been coerced into drinking the Kool-Aid that promotes the aftertaste of its sweeter when your man's not home, a sign that "Willie Lynchism" is still affecting and metastasizing in the culture.

Men are being replaced in the educational system by the thousands as they lay nestled in their beds of mediocrity: after all, "It's a woman's job," they say. While the masses of women are teaching and training the seeds of this generation, men are enlisting as soldiers in basic training and trade in their genius for bootstraps. Men today would rather have their feet on foreign soil, guarding distant lands, while their homes go unguarded.

I am afraid pretty soon the earth will go man-less almost like the masses are going meatless. Before long there will be no Adam (man) in Eden's Garden just mixed up fruits and vegetables. Soon man will be a monument mentioned only in the archives of museums next to the morgue of a distant yesterday. I can't even fathom a man-less world but that's the new series that the world is showcasing on the Jumbo Tron of the mainstream media. I would change the channel but it is playing on every station in a synchronized fashion.

Men, our children don't call us fathers anymore. They address us by our first names almost like we didn't have a major part in their existence. I guess they divorced us when their mothers couldn't get along with us, because that was the song we keep hearing in our subconscious. Who's going to teach our sons the code since we are growing old, void of a voice that was once deep and embedded with the DNA for masculine survival? Will our young men get swept away by the Apple, ask SIRI for directions, Google a video of what I looked like on YouTube, or simply shoot me a text from the place they'll be holding me? Will our daughters Snap Chat us, just see our profiles on Facebook, talk from virtual reality or keep it *almost* real on FaceTime ? Will our woman's hearts still Twitter at the sound of our voices or will she possibly reject my friend request because I show up unknown. Will they still love us or will their emotions be stuck on Pinterest? Will the loves of our lives be able to decipher our direct messages ? Will

MANHANDLED

"Hidden Code Words That Impact Men And The People That Love Them"

they still have us LinkedIn ?

We shouldn't have talked to the Serpent or dare let it speak. This same serpent has set his sights and tricked us for apples. We are most certain the same enemy in Adam's garden planned this. This entire scheme, this entire script that flipped the scenes was aimed at making us man-less.

MY SON SHALL RISE AGAIN

LIKE OVER 72% of African-American children living in the United States (current statistic as of 2016), I was born out-of-wedlock and raised mostly by my single mother. After 21 hours of life-threatening and excruciating labor resulting from breech birth complications, I was born at 4:00 am on September 25, 1976. Upon delivery, my mother told me later that I slipped through both the doctor's and labor nurse's hands, nearly crashing head-first onto the floor. Just in the nick of time, the labor nurse pulled me up by my infant wrist, leaving me in the squatting position with my feet lodged to the floor and my hands lifted up. Little did I know that this bizarre sequence of events would serve as a prophetic omen for the way my life would unfold. As a result of the trauma experienced at childbirth, I was placed inside a neonatal incubator under doctors' care for two weeks.

For my survival and safety, it was important to maintain my environment with precise temperature, humidity, and oxygen

MANHANDLED

"Hidden Code Words That Impact Men And The People That Love Them"

concentration levels. Also during this time, I learned later that my biological father, who had persistently tried to talk my mother into aborting me, arrived at the hospital intoxicated, and walked into our hospital room.

The word *Father* is defined by The Free Dictionary by Farlex as: ***"a man who creates, originates, or founds something.*** "In stark contrast to that definition, here are the first words that proceeded out of my biological father's mouth: ***"This baby is not my son; his complexion is too light and he doesn't look like me at all!"*** By anyone's definition, those are not the words of a true father. Although I was only a couple of days old, and couldn't comprehend the depth of the words my father had spoken over me, his spoken words would nonetheless create a gaping hole within the framework of my life.

My father's initial spoken words released the spirit of denial over my life, and sent me spinning helplessly on the Ferris wheel of rejection. Shortly after being discharged from the hospital, my mother ended her relationship with my father, and I had little or no contact with my dad for many years. Before long, my mother was introduced to another man by a mutual family member. Following several months of dating, he proposed to take my mother's hand in marriage, pledged his undying love for both my mother and me, and vowed to embrace me like his very own son. Determined to rebound from the rejection of her first love, and battling internal apprehension, she accepted his proposal.

Without a moment's pause, they were married by a justice of the peace, and we all moved to another city to begin a brand new life together. Unlike most dramas played out on the big screen, there were no scenes in my life that depicted living "happily ever after". Several years after moving to a neighboring city, my mom gave birth to her second child, and my life immediately took a turn for the worse. My stepfather, the only father figure I had known, began to resent me, and verbally lashed out at me.

Before the age of five, I was called lazy, hardheaded, stupid and crazy, and those were the good days. From the age of six until I turned twelve, my stepfather's rage intensified, and abusive words

MANHANDLED

"Hidden Code Words That Impact Men And The People That Love Them"

were now matched by physical blows to my frail body. Day after day, and night after night, I found myself helpless and painfully trapped behind enemy lines within my own home.

As the years of my childhood passed me by, I grew more accustomed to being my stepfather's punching bag. He often came home mad at the world, and for no apparent reason, punched me in the face until my nose started bleeding. Often during the beatings, my stepdad would grab both of my ankles and dangle me upside down until I wet my clothes in fear. Then he would continue to beat me until he got tired and I could no longer cry. Nonetheless, I still yearned for my stepdad to embrace me as a son, and to feel a father's touch. I was well-acquainted with the love of a God-fearing mother, but had never felt the embrace of a father.

Despite the verbal and physical abuse, I still reached out to my stepfather for love and affirmation, only to have my heart crushed time and time again. The last time my stepfather physically abused me, the pounding was so severe that the scars are still tattooed to my body to this day. At this point, my mother finally had enough and separated from my stepfather for several months. Throughout the six-month separation, my mother continued to pray and speak the prophetic Word of God over my life. Shortly after we (mother, sister and I) moved into my Godmother's apartment, we began praying and calling out to God for healing and restoration. I will never forget feeling the presence of the Holy Spirit as I called out to God to become my father for the first time.

So many times in my childhood I had cried out to God for help from my beatings, rejections, and pain, but this time I embraced God as my Father. Instantly, without hesitation, at the age of twelve, God answered my call, filled me with his precious Holy Spirit, and became the father I was longing for my entire

life. Then God whispered to my spirit these four words that would transform my life forever: **"My *son, you shall rise again*"**.

Immediately, I knew and understood that despite how badly I had been broken, God could still repair me. From the day I embraced God as my father, I was given an internal peace and eternal affirmation from the Holy Spirit that I would rise above all of my

MANHANDLED

"Hidden Code Words That Impact Men And The People That Love Them"

afflictions. God began to reveal to my mother and me that the sequence of events at my birth prophetically symbolized my life; regardless of how severe the events were, I would always land on my feet with my hands raised towards Heaven.

After six months, my mother returned home and the physical abuse from my stepfather stopped; the mental and verbal abuse however, intensified, and continued until I left home for college.

Some years later, my Stepfather was killed in a car accident; just like that, without notice, he was gone. Despite many opportunities, my stepfather never did muster up the courage to apologize to me for the many years of abuse.

Through much travail, God granted to me the grace to forgive my stepfather for all of his abuse, despite the fact that he died without reconciling or taking responsibility for his actions. I am a living witness that Romans 8:28 is not just a biblical cliché; truly, all things good, bad, and, ugly work together for good for those who love God and are called according to His purpose. After embracing

God as my father, He granted my biological father and me a second chance. After several years of no contact with him, my mom called me one afternoon—a time I can remember like it was yesterday.

"Your father just called me," my mother explained, "and said he'd like to speak with you. He wants you to give him a call."

Instantly, I became infuriated. ***"He's a coward!"***, I thought to myself. ***"Why couldn't he call me himself?"*** *"After all,"* I justified pridefully, *"**he was the one who rejected me.**"*

Realizing that my intense feelings would not make me a good driver, I pulled over into a McDonald's parking lot to speak with her. Following my initial outburst, my thoughts deepened, and I asked God (and myself), ***"Why now?"*** and ***"What now?"***

I struggled with these two questions in my heart as my mind dug rapidly through the clutter of pain, rejection, anger, and surprise. I thought I was over it; I thought I had forgiven my father. After all, I was saved, and was now a Pastor, living beyond that pit I had escaped from. ***"I'm okay, I'm okay,"*** I repeatedly told myself. So I thought, until I was confronted with this opportunity to reunite with my father.

MANHANDLED

"Hidden Code Words That Impact Men And The People That Love Them"

Have you ever thought you were healed from a past wound, only to be jolted awake to the harsh reality that it still exists?

The bandages that I had wrapped around the wounds from my father were now unraveling, and the wounds were open and exposed. The truth is that they had never been closed; I just kept them hidden underneath the camouflage of my denial. I turned my focus back to the call with my mother. *"No,"* I said, *"I don't want to speak with my father."*

After our call ended, the next thing I know, I'm crying like a baby in my car in the McDonald's parking lot. I didn't care who saw me, a middle-aged man, weeping in public. See, there was still a battered little boy inside of me, and his tears had been held in for far too long. I *had to* release these bottled-up feelings; they simply had to come out. My crying could no longer be muzzled, as I sobbed uncontrollably. Over an hour passed, and the tears were still coming. It felt like I was suspended in time, crying for every moment I had been without my father. After all of my tears however, I realized that my father had been given plenty of chances in the past to become my dad, and had forfeited them all. No more chances. When I got home, hurt had pushed its way back to the forefront of my heart.

"He isn't really my father anyway," I told my wife, "He's just the sperm donor known as my father!" My wife gently kept reminding me of the truth that my father was still my father despite what he had done to me. After a heated debate about whether I should call my father, my stubbornness kicked in, and I decided not to call him.

Determined to keep my word, I headed to class that night. Then an uncommon thing happened in the midst of something common. In Bible College, we always opened up each class with prayer. This particular night when I walked into class, my instructor immediately turned to the class and said, "I just feel led to pray for the needs of the students tonight. Does anyone have a prayer request?" Students offered their prayer request one by one. Meanwhile, I wrestled over whether I would be completely transparent and ask for prayer regarding my situation. Suddenly, I felt my hand rise, and I opened my mouth and out came all

MANHANDLED

"Hidden Code Words That Impact Men And The People That Love Them"

of my issues. This truly was a miracle, since I was/am a very private person. Not only did my instructor pray for me, but the entire class began to speak prophetic words over my life! Before I knew it, I was feeling lighter and the huge weight of my burden had somehow gotten lifted in the presence of the Lord.

I made up my mind that I was going to adhere to the leading of the Holy Spirit and call my father. I didn't want to hesitate, so during our class break, I called my father right then and there, no time to waste. As soon as the phone rang, my father answered. Breaking the silence, the first words my father uttered were, *"I'm so sorry."* My father apologized for neglecting his responsibilities, and for every indiscretion he had committed. In the spirit of forgiveness, we reconciled after 33 years of being apart!

Regardless of how far I was dropped by life's events, I was never broken beyond repair, because God's hand—symbolized by the labor nurse's hands at my birth—was always lifting me up. I prophesy over each one of you reading this page at this moment, in the face of all the adversity you have experienced in your life, ***"You will rise again"***.

During the Christmas holiday season of 2010, I was faced with the tragic loss of a loved one. My father died suddenly, without warning, and with no time to say goodbye. Now I can only rely on God to bring closure and mend my broken heart.

Believe me, I'm not writing this to play the role of a victim, but inviting you inside my life, so that you may examine the victory I've experienced by having a sincere relationship with Christ. Contrary to popular opinion, bad things can still occur during good times or joyful seasons of our life. In other words, troubled waters can overflow and storms can rain in our life despite a forecast of clear blues skies and sunny conditions. Trust me, it is hard to stand still when you don't know what you're waiting for, or what to do. God desires to teach us how to stand still, wait, and listen to Him.

If you're like me, you need Christ to provide you with the necessary tools to go through every event in life.

MANHANDLED

"Hidden Code Words That Impact Men And The People That Love Them"

"X-Man"

IT'S A SHAME that the same blood which flows from your heart also courses through my veins. As time progressed, I looked more and more like you. I crawled to you, and when I could speak, I called for you. But it seemed like you were never here, man; you were over there, everywhere else, except for here. So I labeled you my **X-MAN**.

There is no pain like living in a day-to-day prison, endlessly bleeding from the cuts of careless rejection. Trapped at life's intersection, parallel to nowhere, across the street from neglect, on the corner of displacement and rejection, resting at the stoplight of anger, and standing still in quicksand. Don't get me wrong, man. I know your old man put the **X** on you. Glory to the Son of Man who took away my **X**, tilted it on its axis, and now it's a cross. Now I'm a new man, lacking, wanting, and needing nothing.

Christ, multiply my spiritual and physical inheritance like the grains of sand. Today I recite truth in the ears of my young man that **X** marks the spot of God's eternal plan.

TONGUE TIED

You Are What You Say!
(Dr. Oliver T. Reid)

I never fathomed that I could have what I say and become what I said. See, under no circumstance did I know the key of choice to succeed or fail was locked securely between my lips. Yes, countless words would slip off the tip of my tongue like a handcrafted paintbrush in the hands of a prolific artist carefully capturing a self-made portrait on multiple blank canvases. Too many days I engaged in careless chatter declaring life to dead things and proclaiming death over a living matter.

The words I verbalized became sentences etched in the manuscript of my life and dictated how my drama would end. Time and time again my stepmother named Society told me to express my thoughts, be blunt to the point, speak precisely what's on my mind, and never hold anything in.

Society nursed me close to her breast and trained me to confess my private thoughts, which in turn wrapped knots around my mentality, and performed frequent eulogies to pending accomplishments. Contrary to popular opinion, talk is not cheap. I truly cashed in on the words I had spoken, within idioms I decide whether to ascend or descend based on how my phrases end and begin.

Remember the tongue can tie one face down, unshackle what was bound, make your low places mountains or mounds, position you on higher or lower ground, turn your bad or good situation around, and flip negativity or positivity upside down. This thing called the tongue can cut like a razor blade on a sharp knife, strike with venomous force like a deadly viper destroying all life, turn unity into strife, and definitely raise or drop a retail price. Tongues can cause your destiny to turn if you don't turn the words you speak around. Untying the tongue takes tremendous tolerance, timing, tact, transparency, training, toiling and temperance.

Conclusion

DISLAMIER

Everything I have shared in this book are powerful tools that help break or decipher codes in men's lives. I've shared from a man's perspective and can't guarantee that what I have shared in this book works for all men. What I can tell you is that if a man is to change he would have to be vested in his own transformation as well as all those around him. I can assure you if you follow these codes outlined in this book and all parties involved seek God's guidance and buy into the concepts change will occur. No two men are alike, but God has encoded the male chromosomes for masculinity. In order for these codes to work, one has to openly and willingly participate. Remember this is a journey you're on with the man in your life. It's not a sprint, but a slow marathon. It is never a dictatorship but a never-ending partnership with an imperfect person working towards change every day. Give the codes time to work. Cover each code in prayer. Don't forget your job is to release the codes not to own it.

Men often fight despite retreating! In other words men and women perceptions are different even though they are one man (mankind) with two different functions they see from two different sides. Yes it is understandable and it could be that he's not equipped to fight on the level you need or he misinterprets where you misinterpret the effort of his fight. What you speak to in a man will unlock or slam close the combination to the treasure of his heart. We must pay attention to see if the words that we speak open or see if we receive a message back saying, "access denied", which means this is not the right set of words to communicate at the time . It doesn't mean it's not the right words it could just be the place of that man's position is not open to receive at that time .

It could also imply that it is simply not the right word for this man. For example if you have an aggressive speaking tone it could be the way you said it not the words in and of themselves. Another example is if you have an aggressive personality or aggressive style; maybe you're very assertive and that man is an introvert.

It will be easy for that man to be distorted or distracted by the style of what you're communicating with him versus the mission

MANHANDLED

"Hidden Code Words That Impact Men And The People That Love Them"

and intent of why you are saying the words that you are speaking.

If you are not conscious of this important point you'll be talking in open sentences but finding yourself living behind closed doors. In other words you would be thinking you're having a conversation but you have not unlocked or access the key to that man. This communication in turn will lead to frustration, feelings of rejection, broken relationships, anger, and the lack of validation.

Discovering the right mixture or communication style and words in which you use is an ongoing journey. It is also a moving target; the words you spoke to a man when you first met him may not be the exact same words you need to speak 20 years from now. It is important to note that men develop and men evolve from one stage in life to another they become wiser, smarter, or even frail, depending on what stage they are in the life cycle.

For instance when you first met your mate you talked about dreams of becoming a successful family; now, three children later, you have a family the conversation must change from the hope of beginning a family to the fact that the family is already here. If you continue to focus on the hope of beginning a family when you have one, you will simply be using the wrong code. A more perfect conversation would be centered around growing those children and sustaining what you already have.

Another thing I want to cover as I close, is that it's very imperative in decoding the man code to allow that man an opportunity to freely express himself without finishing his sentences, thoughts and intents or misinterpreting his actions. Never fail to realize that each man has a code or pattern of communication. It is common for people in the heat of passion to become more concerned about their perceptions and what's actually taking place. It is been scientifically proven that we hear at a faster rate than we speak.

That means during the conversation there is a lot of dead space and a lot of dead time. For example the man could be explaining why he did what he has done and if you're not careful, you will be

MANHANDLED

"Hidden Code Words That Impact Men And The People That Love Them"

waiting on the receiving end, hoping they will "just get to the point" and totally fail to see, hear, and ultimately miss the opportunity to unlock him. To get to the surface and root of the problem was in listening and allowing him to feel and express himself. More often than not, people feel that they are having a conversation with a male factor and is simply a one-sided form of communication. It is so important to look for clues like the man's body language when you are talking and then engaging in conversation. What are his eyes telling you, his voice telling you, what is he not saying because he feels he doesn't have an outlet? What are the barriers? It is imperative to gain the understanding or the fact that men need to feel safe as well as enabled to speak. Ask yourself these questions: am I enabling or disabling the man in my life by the words that I am choosing to speak? One must examine that the code words they say will set the stage of expectation long before they do anything.

Words precede actions and often trigger a response before the intention of the words we speak are made clear. Once you speak a word out it is hard to retract it or define what you really meant by it so choose your words with discretion.

You don't want to release the wrong code to the right man. Better yet you don't want to lock yourself out of an opportunity to make a divine connection or impartation into a man's life because of a bad word choice. Speak life, and unlock the code of the men you love.

TO BE CONTINUED…...

MANHANDLED

"Hidden Code Words That Impact Men And The People That Love Them"

JOURNAL ENTRY PAGE

(Feel free to journal your thoughts and learning experiences by answering the questions below.

🔍 HOW DID YOU FEEL WHEN READING THIS CHAPTER?

_____
_____
_____
_____
_____
_____

🔍 WHAT DID YOU LEARN?

_____
_____
_____
_____
_____
_____

🔍 HOW CAN YOU USE THIS INFORMATION TO HELP SOMEONE ELSE IN LIFE?

_____
_____
_____
_____
_____
_____

🔍 HOW DOES THE CONTENT OF THIS CHAPTER RELATE TO YOUR LIFE EXPIRENCE(S)?

_____
_____
_____
_____
_____
_____

JOURNAL ENTRY PAGE

(Feel free to journal your thoughts and learning experiences by answering the questions below.

🔍 HOW DID YOU FEEL WHEN READING THIS CHAPTER?

_____
_____
_____
_____
_____
_____

🔍 WHAT DID YOU LEARN?

_____
_____
_____
_____
_____
_____

🔍 HOW CAN YOU USE THIS INFORMATION TO HELP SOMEONE ELSE IN LIFE?

_____

_____

_____

_____

_____

_____

🔍 HOW DOES THE CONTENT OF THIS CHAPTER RELATE TO YOUR LIFE EXPIRENCE(S)?

_____

_____

_____

_____

_____

_____

JOURNAL ENTRY PAGE

(Feel free to journal your thoughts and learning experiences by answering the questions below.

🔍 HOW DID YOU FEEL WHEN READING THIS CHAPTER?

🔍 WHAT DID YOU LEARN?

HOW CAN YOU USE THIS INFORMATION TO HELP SOMEONE ELSE IN LIFE?

HOW DOES THE CONTENT OF THIS CHAPTER RELATE TO YOUR LIFE EXPIRENCE(S)?

JOURNAL ENTRY PAGE

(Feel free to journal your thoughts and learning experiences by answering the questions below.

🔍 HOW DID YOU FEEL WHEN READING THIS CHAPTER?

🔍 WHAT DID YOU LEARN?

🔍 HOW CAN YOU USE THIS INFORMATION TO HELP SOMEONE ELSE IN LIFE?

_____
_____
_____
_____
_____
_____

🔍 HOW DOES THE CONTENT OF THIS CHAPTER RELATE TO YOUR LIFE EXPIRENCE(S) ?

_____
_____
_____
_____
_____
_____

ACCEPTING CHRIST IS EASY AS SAYING OUR ABC'S

At the conclusion of our awesome journey together, I want to extend to you an opportunity and a personal invitation to make, if you have not already, one of the greatest choices one can ever make. The simple choice to accept Jesus Christ into your heart is as easy as A, B, and C. Please don't wait until tomorrow. Today is the day of salvation. "For He says, in time of favor (of an assured welcome) I have listened to and heeded your call, and I have helped you on the day of deliverance (the day of salvation). Behold, now is truly the time for a gracious welcome and acceptance [of you from God]; behold, now is the day of salvation." (II Corinthians 6:2 AMP)

A. All you have to do is Acknowledge (admit, accept, allow, and agree) that you need Jesus Christ in your life and heart. Acknowledge that Christ gave his life for you. (Romans 10:9 AMP)

B. Next, simply Believe (adhere to, trust in, and rely on the truth) that God raised Him from the dead, and you will be saved. (Romans 10:9 AMP)

C. Finally, all you have to do is Confess (announce, affirm, pronounce, and admit) what you believe. Confess with your lips that Jesus is Lord! (Romans 10:9 AMP)

You are now saved, washed completely from your sins and forgiven for all of the wrongs done in the past. The angels in heaven are, at this very second, throwing a party in your honor. Congratulations on becoming a member of the prestigious and elite group called, the *"Body of Christ."*

About the Author

Dr. Reid has used God's blessings and favor upon his life in the marketplace, as Founder of ECKLESIA Professional Development Center in 2001, and Founder of M.I.N.D. Consulting in 2007. Dr. Reid provides mental health and consulting services through his companies, and is also a seasoned trainer, motivational speaker and writer.

Dr. Reid is an international best-selling author. His first book, *Don't Press Fast Forward*, was released in 2010, and four other books have been released: *Spiritual GPS*, *Your Ministry is not Impossible*, *Nine Keys to Keeping a Vision Fresh*, and *Words from the Low Place*.

Using his God-given passion to teach, Dr. Reid has also developed a series of empowerment workshops and conferences. In addition, Dr. Reid launched the I Am a Solution Consulting Firm, LLC for empowering men to change the world.

A native of Charlotte, North Carolina, Dr. Reid is married to Miatta Reid and a proud father. He graduated from Winston Salem State University with a BA/BS degree in History and Sociology, and earned a Bachelors and Master's in Theology from Life Christian University. Dr. Oliver Reid received his PhD in Christian Counseling from Clarity International University in 2013.

You can connect with Apostle Dr. Oliver T. Reid at the links below.

yoursolutioncoach@gmail.com
www.iamasolutionconsultingfirmllc.com

DR. OLIVER T. REID

Available Now!

DON'T PRESS FAST FORWARD
"PROPHETIC BLUE PRINTS TO WEATHERING THE STORM"

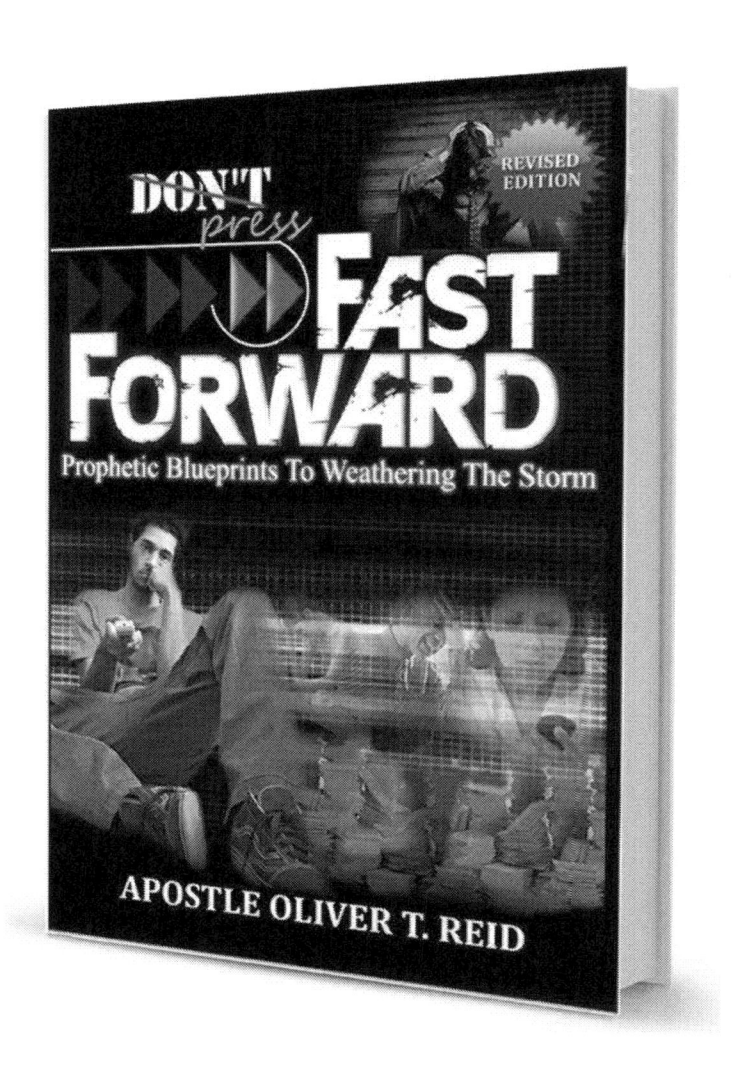

MANHANDLED

"Hidden Code Words That Impact Men And The People That Love Them"

WORDS FROM THE LOW PLACE " YOUR LOWEST FOR GOD'S HIGHEST"

The Book That Breaks Barriers Simply By The Power Of Testimonies!DAILY

DR. OLIVER T. REID

DAILY DEVOTIONAL AND INSTRUCTIONS

MANHANDLED

"Hidden Code Words That Impact Men And The People That Love Them"

UPCOMING BOOK RELEASES FROM DR. OLIVER T. REID

Solutions in
60 MINUTES
With Dr. Oliver T. Reid
Your Solution Coach
I am a Solution
The Branding gospel
OTR MINISTRIES INTERNATIONAL
www.i-am-asolution.com

MANHANDLED

"Hidden Code Words That Impact Men And The People That Love Them"

Dr. Oliver T. Reid

RESTLESS
Freeing Yourself From The Straitjacket of Offense

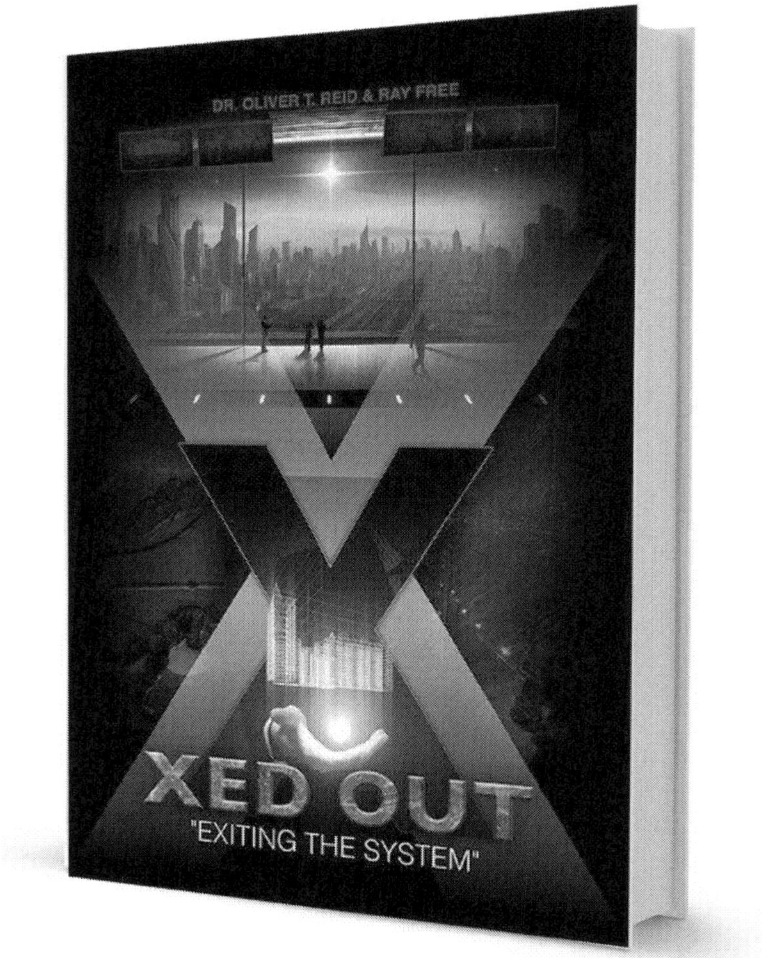
DR. OLIVER T. REID & RAY FREE
XED OUT
"EXITING THE SYSTEM"

MANHANDLED

"Hidden Code Words That Impact Men And The People That Love Them"

DR. OLIVER T. REID

MANHANDLED

"Hidden Code Words That Impact Men And The People That Love Them"

SOLUTIONS
IN SECONDS
Periscope
YOUR SOLUTION COACH
@INSOLUTIONMODE
I am a
Solution
The Branding gospel
OTR MINISTRIES INTERNATIONAL

MANHANDLED

"Hidden Code Words That Impact Men And The People That Love Them"

Be Sure And Visit:

www.iamasolutionconsultingfirmllc.com
For More Info & Updates

Made in United States
Orlando, FL
04 February 2023